Chipmunks as Pets.

Chipmunk Owner's Manual.

Chipmunk keeping, pros and cons, care, housing, diet, training and health.

By

Roger Rumford

Contents

Introduction

The idea of domesticating animals is not new; we have been creating a chain of connections with several species in the animal kingdom for the purpose of peaceful coexistence. History may have taught modern man to breed cattle, horses and poultry for personal consumption and profit, yet our relationship with animals today has become more complex, even emotional.

We now view animals not only as a source of profit, but also as a source of love and companionship. Through our discovery of new species and their natures, we have also modified the concept of domestication, with exotic animals being domesticated with as much enthusiasm - and considerable success - as the conventional ones. What is fascinating, however, is that people tend to have varied preferences when asked to select an animal they would like for companionship.

For some, the perfect animal companion is one that is energetic, affectionate and boisterous. Those with a quiet demeanor may prefer an animal that is well behaved, disciplined and calm. Some may describe their perfect companions to be those who swim behind large glass enclosures, providing tranquility and beauty. Others still may chose to bring home those pets that can be trained and raised for long-term profits. If you belong to that elite group of people who seek a close relationship with their pets within the mammalian kingdom, and enjoy the company of lively, curious animals, chipmunks may be the ideal pets for you.

Of the 25 species of chipmunks that are found around the world, only a handful have been observed to be suitable for taming and domestication. The limit posed by legal laws and the aversion towards domestication displayed by many chipmunk breeds makes it additionally challenging to find the ideal breed. After a prolonged history of exposure to humans, however, Siberian chipmunks found in Asian countries, along with some varieties of the Eastern chipmunk found in the North American continent have been found to be most prone to taming.

Curious and energetic by nature, these members of the rodent family prefer to spend their existence engaging in foraging and storage behaviors, with some hours of the day devoted to exercise and habitat management. Do not mistake their tiny sizes for a docile nature; these mammals have highly independent and aggressive natures and can spring into defensive attacks if a threat is sensed.

A quality that makes the chipmunk a prized pet is its ability to form lasting bonds with its caregiver, if given proper care and attention. Provided it is housed in a large enclosure that promotes exercise and movement and receives plenty of food for immediate feeding and future storage, your chipmunk will live a content life and provide companionship for up to eight years.

These omnivorous creatures have generous appetites and a virtually unquenchable thirst. They are also prone to bursts of aggression and hostility during the winter months, and may become easily agitated. On the other hand, tame chipmunks also make for intimate companions who are content to perch on the shoulders of the caregivers they trust.

These independent mammals are of robust health as well, rarely succumbing, if ever, to life-threatening diseases and illnesses. Common health-related ailments may include superficial wounds and injuries sustained during fights, or an infection contracted due to inhospitable housing conditions.

The health and well being of chipmunks in captivity is largely reliant on the kind of living environment you can provide. In favorable and nurturing environments, chipmunks can also be relatively easy and rewarding to breed, whether for personal use or for profit. It is no wonder, then, that chipmunks are enthusiastically given a home by anyone who is lucky to encounter one of these.

If you too wish to bring home a chipmunk, you will gain deeper insight into its world through this book - from its natural settings, to its behavioral patterns. You will also be guided through every stage of owning a chipmunk, from initial thought to eventual raising. With a positive attitude and a dedicated spirit, you can work past the challenges that come with housing a chipmunk, and integrate them seamlessly into your life.

Chapter 1: Meet the Chipmunks

Chipmunks are often characterized by their seemingly harmless and pleasing appearance - with furry tails, tiny striped bodies and comically large teeth and eyes, chipmunks are mistakenly assumed to possess a cheerful disposition and friendly demeanor. In reality, the chipmunk, though tiny in size, is aggressive by nature, and prefers to spend its days in isolation. Having evolved as diurnal forest creatures that rely on natural sources for foraging and survival, chipmunks are among the more visible members of the rodent family, with other members comprising such species as hamsters, rats, guinea pigs and chinchillas.

1.   Natural History

Chipmunks have been classified into three main categories on the basis of their geographic location, with each category housing its own subspecies of chipmunks - The Tamias Striatus or Eastern Chipmunk, the Neo Tamias Striatus or Western chipmunk, and the Eutamias Sibiricus, also known as the Siberian chipmunk. While the Siberian chipmunk is the sole member of its family, the Eastern and Western families include a total of 24 different breeds, including Townsend chipmunks, least chipmunks, Durango chipmunks, cliff chipmunks and red-tailed chipmunks.

Chipmunks are also distinguished by their need for hibernation and torpor in the winter months. Storing large reserves of nuts and seeds within a complex maze of interconnecting underground tunnels, chipmunks spend the cold months in a state of elongated stupor, only emerging towards the advent of spring to mate and breed.

With a diverse array of vocal abilities, chipmunks use an intensive vocabulary of chirps and calls to communicate with each other. Distinct sound patterns are employed to signal dominance over an occupied territory, concern over invasion from a larger predator, or even to entice suitors during the breeding season. Female chipmunks, upon impregnation, birth a litter containing an average of 4 to 6 chipmunks and provide care for the young until they are physically independent.

Content to spend their days looking for new food sources and breeding at appropriate times, chipmunks in the wild have been observed to have a lifespan of 2 to 5 years, while those chipmunks raised in captivity have lived up to 10 years.

2. Physical Appearance

Young chipmunks are born hairless, blind and without any sense of motor control. Weighing less than an ounce at birth, they develop fur and stripes within the first two weeks of life, with colorings becoming prominent by the sixth week of development. During the fourth week, young chipmunks - also known as puppies - will receive such abilities as sight, aided by the complete opening of their ears. Birthed and nursed in underground burrows by their mothers for the first few weeks, chipmunks only emerge from their underground nesting spots once they have transitioned from their puppy state into an independent, adolescent state.

The average adult chipmunk measures between 2 and 6 inches, with the least chipmunk breed being the smallest of the chipmunks. From the body extends a furry tail that measures around 3 inches in length. With such tiny dimensions, the average chipmunk rarely weighs over half-a-kilogram (1.3 pounds). Often confused for squirrels, chipmunks are easily distinguished by their elongated front teeth, smaller size, pointed ears and distinct coloring patterns. Their bodies are often covered with a soft, furry coat that consists of a base pigment and a pattern of stripes that run down the length of the chipmunk's back.

Chipmunk breeds and common color varieties

With variations found in different breeds, chipmunks will usually be found to posses fur in shades of yellow, gray and brown, with white and black stripes streaking the length of their torso. The color of their fur is determined by the permutation and combination of genes responsible for pigmentation and coloring supplied to the chipmunk by its parents.

Genetic traits such as eye color, texture of the coat and physical size are programmed into the DNA of each cell in the chipmunk's body. The DNA comes from their mother and father.

Most chipmunks possess a brown or gray dominant coloring trait, white being its submissive counterpart. Commonly seen among chipmunks of the western and Siberian variety, brown/gray chipmunks, also known as Agouti chipmunks, are among the most commonly found variety of rodent. Agouti chipmunks can be identified by the brown or gray fur on their head, along with a large gray patch on the neck. Stripes in Agouti chipmunks often begin in dark markings from the shoulder area, lightening to shades of copper or ginger as they reach the tail.

In the event that a chipmunk's coloring trait is determined by the victory of a submissive trait over a dominant one, the resulting chipmunks, upon attaining fur, will spot hair that is white in color and streaked with a pattern of stripes in brown/gray. Also known as Dilute chipmunks, these rodents should not be confused with albino chipmunks, who may have similarly white fur, but will also have red eyes as opposed to the chipmunk's large black ones. Brown stripes, though present on a Dilute chipmunk's body, may not always be visible from a distance.

Genetic traits such as color of the fur may often manifest itself in more than one result; though Agouti and Dilutes may be the most popular varieties, such natural phenomena as cross-breeding or the emergence of a highly recessive trait may result in chipmunks developing a coat in hues other than brown/grey and white. Several species of chipmunks, though less common than the Agouti or Dilute breeds, can also be found in varying shades of copper or even black.

Cinnamon chipmunks are chipmunks whose coat has developed a stronger ginger tint than its Agouti cousin. Though their coloring may make their coats lighter than Agouti chipmunks, Cinnamon chipmunks possess a coat that is more vibrant than the greyish-brown hue of their counterparts. It is this physical distinction that has prompted several breeders to attempt efforts that considerably raise the population of Cinnamon chipmunks bred in captivity.

Another extremely rare variety of chipmunk, the black chipmunk, has found itself on the receiving end of attention from professional breeders and enthusiasts. Black chipmunks receive their color through an extremely rare result achieved during the fusing of parent DNA - a result that is being considered in academic fields to be the polar opposite of a combination that breeds Dilute chipmunks.

3.   Natural Range and Habitat

Except for the Siberian chipmunks, all other breeds of chipmunks can be found within the North American continent. Spanning the length of the terrain, from the northern parts of Canada to the central parts of Mexico, North America is home to 24 different chipmunk breeds. Their Siberian cousins, on the other hand, are found in the Asian and eastern European continents, in such countries as Japan, South Korea, Russia, China and the United Kingdom (although largely in captivity).

Owing to the differences in geographical conditions, climates and the resulting adaption chipmunks have made during the course of evolution, chipmunk breeds in North America are largely classified into two subgroups: Eastern chipmunks, who inhabited the eastern parts of the United States and Canada, and the Western chipmunks who can be found in the western areas of the United States, Canada and Mexico.

Eastern chipmunks are known to prefer burrowing houses under the earth's surface, tend to avoid high perches and possess aggressive natures. Western chipmunks, on the other hand, have been studied to show a preference for the higher, inaccessible cliffs and rocky areas in their habitat. While observed to be less aggressive than their eastern counterparts, Western chipmunks prefer to spend their days in isolation and can be difficult to spot in public places.

Siberian chipmunks, on the other hand, seem to possess a range of personality traits that combine those of the Eastern and Western breeds. While Siberian chipmunks burrow under the ground to build their tunnels, they are just as likely to spend their waking days climbing high perches and housing nut caches in abandoned nests and crevices. Siberian chipmunks have also been studied to possess a less aggressive nature than their eastern cousins, and a less withdrawn nature than their western cousins.

Within their natural surroundings, most eastern and Siberian chipmunks settle amidst areas with ample floor cover and objects that offer protection from predators and harsh climatic conditions such as logs, tree stumps, shrubs and rocks. No matter what the breed, all chipmunks find ideal spots for housing, food storage and hibernation within densely green woodlands, deciduous forests and brush lands. Those chipmunks that have been exposed to urbanization and human settlements in sparsely forested areas have also been found to build their homes in such spaces as parks and hedges.

To facilitate safe housing and secure storage for nuts for the winter months, chipmunks create their homes by burrowing and digging an intricate and extensively laid-out network of tunnels and burrows, as deep as 3 feet below the earth's surface. Extra-attentive to such circumstances as destruction of the storage area, and possible invasion from predators, chipmunks build two types of homes that serve different purposes. One home consists of a group of temporary burrows and storage cubbies built at a shallow depth. These burrows are mainly used to store food that has been gathered from farther foraging points, until it can be transferred to the second, more permanent home. This second home serves as the chipmunk's hibernation space in the winter, and is planned and constructed in a series of interconnecting tunnels that house food storage burrows at accessible points.

4.   Commonly found Chipmunk varieties

Eastern Chipmunk

Among the most commonly found chipmunk species in the United States is the Eastern chipmunk. These rodents are found inhabiting woody areas, valleys enriched with rivers, and urban settlements with similar setups. Eastern chipmunks feed largely on fruits, seeds and nuts. Known to be largely solitary and territorial by nature, they make their intentions to other animals known through a series of distinct vocalizations. While the male members of this variety are known to be particularly aggressive, the females display their dominant traits by taking many male partners during their lifetime.

Least Chipmunk

The Least chipmunk is probably so-named due to its significantly tiny size, definitely smaller than other chipmunk varieties. Preferring the safety of heights to the predatory approaches of terrestrial housing, Least chipmunks inhabit boreal and temperate forested regions, building their nests in spots high above the forest floor. Least chipmunks make the most of food resources available in their environment and feed on fruits, nuts, berries, local grasses, fungi and snails. Personality-wise, Least chipmunks are probably the most maternal, with mothers caring for their young for up to 60 days.

Red-tailed chipmunk

The Red-tailed chipmunk can most commonly be found scampering about the densely covered coniferous forests of the Alberta and British Columbia provinces of Canada. Feeding on locally available nuts and berries for sustenance, Red-tailed chipmunks are probably best known for their peculiar "sand-bathing" method of grooming. While sand bathing, this variety of chipmunk can be spotted diving headfirst into the sand, and then rolling about on its back from side-to-side.

Townsend chipmunk

Townsend chipmunks, just like their Red-tailed cousins, prefer the dense cover that coniferous forests provide, showing a special preference for the hardwood forests in the British Columbia province in the western part of Canada. These chipmunks also exhibit some of the behavioral traits that their Eastern chipmunk cousins do, by way of displaying exaggerated aggression, a strong territorial instinct and possessing a solitary temperament. Townsend chipmunks, however, have also been observed to show a strong sense of loyalty to other members of their species, especially in times of trouble. They warn their community members of approaching or impending threat with a series of sharp and distinct vocalizations.

Cliff chipmunk

Cliff chipmunks, as its name would suggest, are found to be most comfortable inhabiting the rocky, cliff terrain in the northern parts of Mexico. A large part of their dict includes pine seeds, acorns and juniper berries. Mostly possessing a shy disposition, Cliff chipmunks are content to spend their days around their den - a space they are highly territorial about. When threatened, these shy rodents can quickly turn aggressive and fierce.

Durango chipmunk

Durango chipmunks call the regions between South Chihuahua and west-central Durango, as well as the southeast parts of

Coahuila in Mexico, their home. Sharing the shy disposition of their Cliff chipmunk cousins, this variety shows a preference for the densely covered pine or oak forests in the territory. They prefer to build their homes in inconspicuous areas on the forest floor, such as a rock formation, inside a cozy log or amidst a heap of environmental litter. It is this desire for secretive habitats, along with a withdrawing nature, that has made the Durango chipmunk relatively hard to spot and observe for study.

Siberian chipmunk

The Siberian chipmunk may be the only species of chipmunk found in the Asian and European terrains, but it is a species that compensates for its scarcity in variety by possessing a vast territory. This type of chipmunk is indigenous to such countries as China, North and South Korea, Japan, and the northern parts of Russia. In these areas, Siberian chipmunks make their homes in temperate forest areas, rocky regions and urban buildings and settlements with equal ease.

The Siberian chipmunk availability in the eastern parts of Europe could be attributed to the close borders shared with Russia that the chipmunks cross with little concern. Lenient import regulations and licenses in many countries to own these rodents also makes Siberian chipmunks a common sight in European countries.

Siberian chipmunks have a diverse appetite, consuming everything from fruits and vegetables to grains and seeds, even making a meal out of small insects, lizards and birds. But their most distinguishing feature, perhaps, is their affinity for grooming and cleanliness. Siberian chipmunks can often be spotted indulging in bathing and grooming rituals, and seem to enjoy grooming their siblings and group members as well.

5.   Feeding Habits

Chipmunks are omnivorous by nature, feeding off of all available food resources in their immediate environment that can be grasped within their paws and broken down with their teeth. Nuts, seeds, fruits, edible flowers and plants, along with the odd worm, snail, bug or small bird comprise most of the chipmunks' diet in the wild. Depending on their geographic location, chipmunks may also collect such foods as acorns, berries, and even corn kernels.

Certain varieties of fungi also make up an important part of the chipmunks' nutritional intake. False fungi such as truffles, and other edible varieties such as button mushrooms are rich sources of vitamin D and are essential for the absorption of calcium and the development of bones and teeth.

Chipmunks seem to have a particular fondness for nuts of any variety, and will collect them by the dozens for future storage. It is not just nuts, but also other food sources that are picked for storage and use in the winter months. Chipmunks spend about three to four months in winter hibernating in their underground burrows, and require a vast reserve of foods that do not spoil easily. Beechnuts and acorns, in particular, are considered prized winter food sources.

It is this need for a healthy supply of winter feed that causes chipmunks to assess food sources not only for their immediate nutritional value, but also for their long-term viability. When an abundant food source, such as a beechnut tree with freshly fallen nuts is found, chipmunks will make several trips between the food source and their underground burrows, stuffing up to 30 nuts in their cheek pouches for each trip. Hard at work in the months leading to winter, chipmunks can comfortably store away between 5000 and 6000 nuts in spots of their choosing.

Chipmunks and scatter hoarding

As foraged food forms the primary source of survival for chipmunks in the winter months, they are prone to becoming exceptionally territorial and possessive of their dens, burrows and food supply. Not only do they become hostile towards other chipmunks and animals that try to forage for food from their source, but they also become paranoid about other animals stealing from their stashed-away food reserve. In order to ensure that they don't run out of food during the winter, chipmunks engage in a foraging and storage behavior known as scatter hoarding.

The process of scatter hoarding is carried out in three phases - collecting, sorting, and hoarding. During the first stage, chipmunks scour a range of locations in their natural surroundings, looking for acceptable foods such as nuts, berries, fungi and fruit. These foods are often collected and hidden away in temporary storage burrows located close to the food source. Once their temporary caches are filled, chipmunks visit each storage unit to begin phase two of the process.

During this stage, collected food is evaluated for its long-term durability. If food sources as perishable, chipmunks will either eat them immediately, or store them for use in the immediate future. Other foods, such as nuts, seeds and acorns, are then sorted into piles that either will be stored in the hibernation chambers, or will be hidden away for emergencies - phase three of the scatter hoarding process.

Scatter hoarding, as a behavior pattern, is essential for chipmunks that live in the wild. Surrounded by competitors for shared food sources, chipmunks also risk losing their food reserves to such events as unnaturally lengthy winters, deforestation, urbanization or floods. On a smaller scale, their dens may be invaded by larger animals, may be found and stolen from by other chipmunks, or may even decay prematurely. Backup food supplies help chipmunks navigate unforeseen conditions that may last days, weeks or even months.

6.   Reproductive Cycle

The reproductive cycle of chipmunks begins with the ending of the winter season, between the months of January and March. Female chipmunks have been observed to enter a state of heat earlier than their male counterparts, and commence mating rituals by calling to male suitors with a series of calls. The male chipmunks become sexually active within the next two weeks, and begin their pursuit of the right female mate for reproduction.

It is the female chipmunks that are prone to taking on multiple partners when they ovulate. In a large community, it is the dominant female who receives the first choice of mate, and the male chipmunks engage in competitive scuffles to win this esteemed position. In smaller groups, chipmunks may pair up, interact and mate without any prolonged hostility; aggressive behaviors are common, but not always expected.

The female chipmunk remains in a state of heat for about 7 hours, during which she either mates several times with a single partner, or moves on to other partners if the first male has become exhausted or bored. Once this period ends, the sperm deposited by the male will take between 10 and 15 days to fertilize the egg and deposit the resulting zygote in the uterus. The gestation period in female chipmunks lasts between 27 and 31 days, and ends with the birth of a litter containing between two and nine puppies.

Depending on the breed of chipmunks, and the climatic conditions of their geographical locations, some chipmunks, such as the Eastern and Siberian chipmunks, may undergo another breeding cycle in the late summer months between July and September. The female chipmunks from such species as Western chipmunks may even birth their litter only in the late summer months, reserving the entirety of the winter months for hibernation in extremely cold areas.

Chipmunk babies are born without hair or eyes, measure about 2.5 inches (64 mm) in length, and weight not more than 3 grams (0.1 oz.). Stripes and fur appear on the babies' bodies between the second and fourth week, while they regain complete use of their eyes and ears by the age of four weeks. Once they are weaned off their mother's milk within their underground burrows, chipmunks emerge to the earth's surface at the age of five or six weeks, and learn adult behaviors. Upon attaining independence, offspring often separate from their mothers and venture out to build their own housing networks in surrounding areas. The mother, on her part, either prepares for hibernation, or for another breeding cycle.

With an average lifespan of two to five years in the wild, most chipmunks attain sexual maturity at the age of ten months. Due to the cyclical nature of their breeding cycles and their short life spans, chipmunks will often engage in their own breeding rituals within a year of their birth.

7.   Chipmunks and their role in the Ecology

As inhabitants of such ecologically rich environments as deciduous forests and woodlands, chipmunks play an important part in helping facilitate a natural maintenance of ecological order. As omnivorous creatures, chipmunks feed on a variety of food sources, ranging from nuts and seeds, to fungi, worms and snails. Their preference for such tiny insects as worms, ants, and spiders helps to prevent these populations from reproducing beyond control. Chipmunks also feed on small mice, lizards and other small animals that may be viewed as pests in an urban landscape.

An abundant supply of nuts and seeds in their diet also promotes such environmentally friendly activities as seed dispersal. When scattered by a large population across a cultivable areas, chipmunks, through their droppings, can help plant germinated seeds and encourage afforestation, albeit in a small way.

Chapter 2: Keeping Chipmunks as Pets

1.   Nature of Chipmunks as Pets

Their tiny size and colorful, furry appearance may deceive many aspiring caregivers into believing that chipmunks require little space and attention in order to thrive. Chipmunks, however, have been classified as exotic pets with good reason. An exotic animal is so labeled when it demands specific care, housing and handling techniques. Chipmunks fulfill these requisites by requiring tall, spacious cages to wander in, a varied diet to maintain their health, and precise behavioral treatment for lifelong bonding.

By nature, chipmunks are known to be curious and playful, with a penchant for exploring every nook and cranny of the available environment. This inquisitive nature, however, should not be mistaken for friendliness; many chipmunks may take weeks, even months to domesticate. Until you can forge a relationship of trust with your pet, the chipmunk will resist any attempts at being touched, held or grabbed. With proud, independent personalities, chipmunks may also never entirely become comfortable around your presence, and may have to be left undisturbed.

Despite their independent natures, chipmunks can also be very needy once they bond with their caregivers. In the wild, chipmunks rely on available resources for nutrition and shelter. With timely feeding habits, and a tendency to store excess food away for winter months, it becomes the caregiver's responsibility to ensure that the dietary needs of their pets are met. Care also needs to be taken on behalf of the chipmunk to ensure that all elements in the cage are compatible with the animal's health and safety.

Apart from conditions that promote physical well being, chipmunks also require daily interaction with their caregivers in order to maintain a healthy relationship. Periods of extended neglect may revert your chipmunk back to its wild state, or may cause it stress and sadness. Chipmunks are also diurnal in nature, and are active during the early hours of the day. In order to successfully bond with your chipmunks, you will have to ensure that your daily schedules coincide with the waking hours of your pet; should you work during the day, it may be best to consider nocturnal pets such as sugar gliders or chinchillas.

If the exact care standards required by chipmunks cannot be met, it is best to re-think your decision to house chipmunks, whether for companionship or profit. On the other hand, if you sustain a lifestyle that can comfortably incorporate a pet as demanding as a chipmunk, you may find that they make for entertaining, amusing and rewarding pets.

2.   Advantages of Chipmunks as Pets

As exotics, chipmunks may not have the universal appeal that dogs and cats command. They demand exact living, behavioral, dietary and health conditions in order to thrive, and take relatively longer to tame than other popular pet species. For those who follow a routine that complements the animal's diurnal nature and can make the commitment, however, raising pet chipmunks can turn into a therapeutic and rewarding experience. Despite their slightly fussy natures, chipmunks can be advantageous to their caregivers in the following ways:

• Diurnal by nature, chipmunks are active by day and asleep during the night hours, making them easy to bond with if you work from home or are free during the day.

• While in their cage, they are extremely playful and are always entertaining to watch. They can be tamed and once you bond with your chipmunks, you can also expect them to be equally playful with you.

• Chipmunks are not only clean, but also relatively odorless pets to have around the house, unlike other rodents such as sugar gliders and ferrets (who possess musk glands which emit intense and not particularly pleasant odors).

• Among the cleanest of the rodent bunch, chipmunks may require little or no intensive grooming from you (such grooming needs are reserved for rodents like the chinchilla).

• Chipmunks also possess a fairly high level of intelligence, and can be trained to respond to calls, along with being easy to condition with positive reinforcement. With time and confidence, and depending on their individual personality, your chipmunk may also learn a little trick or two from you.

• Chipmunks are hardy little creatures, with immune systems that can resist most infections - health problems, if any, will often result from misaligned teeth, or wounds and bites sustained from injuries.

• When compared to many other rodents, chipmunks live a relatively long life of 5 to 8 years in captivity, sometimes even living out a complete decade. This longevity of existence makes them ideal pet for those who become quickly attached to their pets and cannot part with them early.

3.   Disadvantages of Chipmunks as Pets

Among those who have not raised a chipmunk or any exotic as a pet before, it is a common misconception that the small, cuddly creatures are low-maintenance and require little care. This harbored notion, however, could not be further from the truth. As is common with all exotics, chipmunks, too, display behavioral patterns that are different from other conventional pets such as dogs, cats, rabbits or horses. They are less likely to adapt their lifestyle to suit yours; rather it is you whose schedule will have to complement the chipmunk's in order for it to survive. As companionable as they can be in the home of the right owner, here are some of the ways that chipmunks could become a disadvantage to unprepared or unwilling owners:

• Chipmunks can be very needy as pets. Apart from timely feeding and health checkups, you will also have to spend at least an hour playing with the pet each day, as prolonged distance from the owner may cause the rodent to revert back to its wild state.

• They demand a lot of attention from caregivers, especially as babies. The amount of time you spend holding and playing with your pet affects how early and how firmly the pet will bond with you.

• Even though they may be needy, chipmunks are also fiercely independent, preferring to be touched or held only when they please. Despite plenty of attention and playtime devoted towards your pet, the chipmunk may still be averse to your touch, or may resist being held.

• Personality-wise, chipmunks are rarely shy or withdrawing. Pet owners often narrate tales of the chipmunks regularly displaying varying degrees of dominance and aggression towards other mates or the caregiver themselves, based on their individual personalities.

• Chipmunks are known to nip or bite other cage mates, or even their caregiver. It must be noted, however, that chipmunks will seldom bite without reason - if they do, it is most often an instinctual response to being held or touched.

• If you are looking for a quiet pet that keeps to themselves, do not be fooled by the chipmunk's cute appearance and small size. Mischievous by nature, they can be relatively destructive when let outside the cage. They are also very energetic, and will need plenty of physical stamina on your part to keep up with them.

• They can also be stubborn pets that resist a firm hand, making their training somewhat exhausting for the caregiver.

• Requiring time for feeding, play, exercise and bonding, caring for chipmunks can be a time-consuming affair and may leave you with little free time to yourself.

• Even though there are plenty of success stories among people who have raised chipmunks, owing to the individualistic personality of the rodent, they may never completely become friendly towards you, despite your best efforts.

4.   Ideal age of the Chipmunks during purchase

As members of the mammalian family, chipmunk puppies rely on their mother's milk and warmth for growth and development for up to the eighth week, at which point they progress to independently foraged solid foods. However, as exotics with individualistic personalities and a need for taming, potential caregivers have the best chances of bonding with their new pets between the fourth and sixth week of their birth. As a potential pet owner, it is your ability and commitment towards being a caregiver that determines the right age of the pet at the time of purchase.

If you choose to bring home a chipmunk between the ages of four and six weeks, such responsibilities as providing puppy milk replacer every few hours, weaning the puppy off milk and onto solid foods and teaching foraging behavior should be prioritized. Chipmunk mothers use the first eight weeks to raise their offspring into fully developed independent animals - if you cannot provide this maternal care, it is best that you acquire an older pet for yourself.

Many exotic pet owners and potential caregivers choose to purchase chipmunks from reputed breeders and fanciers, as they provide chipmunks that have already been tamed and trained to an extent. In addition, regardless of your preferences, a breeder or fancier may not sell a chipmunk to you before they have been weaned successfully. Most chipmunks sold by private breeders are usually only advertised to potential buyers from eight weeks of age.

Ultimately, it is the amount of committed time you can devote towards raising a pet that will determine the ideal age of the chipmunk at the time of purchase. For those who look for a chipmunk with a developed personality and abilities who can still be taught a trick or two, it may be best to choose one between the age of eight and ten weeks.

5.   Housing multiple chipmunks and gender roles

It is a common misconception that chipmunks, as tiny creatures, will require little space, food and a relatively laidback caregiving approach to thrive - one that leads many potential new caregivers to assume that they can take on a larger group of chipmunks with comfort. Housing chipmunks together, however, is a delicate matter that is impacted by such factors as gender differences, age of the cage mates, interpersonal relations and even time of the year.

Along with providing exact primary needs such as food, shelter and rest, a chipmunk's social and emotional needs will also need to be addressed. Chipmunks require some form of interpersonal interaction on a daily basis for their health and wellbeing. If you can devote ample time each day towards playing and bonding with your chipmunk, it may not miss a cage mate except during the breeding season.

On the other hand, if you acquire a young chipmunk from a larger group of siblings and cage mates, it may miss the constant companionship and may become stressed as a result. Therefore, to help make your decision, it is best to have a little knowledge of the dynamics that chipmunks share with each other when housed together in captivity.

Siblings who have been raised together make for the best cage mates - they are happy to share a common space and have little or no compatibility issues. It is wiser, however, to house siblings of the same sex together, whether in pairs or larger groups, than raise a brother and sister in the same cage, in order to avoid such issues as in breeding.

It is not only the relationship of the chipmunks that impacts their compatibility, but also the ratio of males and females housed within the same space. Female chipmunks tend to command the attention of the entire group when in heat, forcing males to compete with each other for the opportunity to mate. If there are fewer females than males in the cage, breeding season may quickly escalate from healthy competition into a furry bloodbath. Ideally, a proportion of two females for every male has been observed to be the minimum requirement to maintain relative harmony during the breeding season.

Your ultimate purpose behind housing and caring for chipmunks also impacts the number of pets you choose to bring home. If you only seek companionship with no intention of breeding chipmunk babies, a pair of same-sex chipmunks, related or otherwise, will get along in relative harmony. In the absence of a female, male chipmunks tend to get along splendidly.

If you do wish to breed the chipmunks for hobby or profit in the long-term, it is wise to invest in a small group of 2-3 female chipmunks, with a viable unrelated male housed in the same cage. Not only will the male chipmunk face no competition at the time of mating, he may also impregnate more than one female member in the group. In addition, female chipmunks tend to form extremely close bonds, and may also help the impregnated chipmunks rear her babies after birth.

Chapter 3: Pet Chipmunks and Social Considerations

As exotic pets, chipmunks will require a detailed list of housing, dietary and health conditions to be met in order to thrive and build a lasting bond with their caregiver. Providing such conditions may not always be feasible for a potential pet owner. A captive chipmunk will require a large room outside the cage for exercise and playtime, will need to be interacted with on a daily basis and will need to be handled in the right way by every member of the family.

With diurnal natures and a tendency to hibernate in the winter months, caregivers will also have to ensure that their lifestyles are compatible with the life cycle of their pets.

While fulfilling such prerequisites may help a chipmunk thrive in captivity, this rigid lifestyle will greatly impact the lives of those housed in the same vicinity as the pet. Therefore, it becomes additionally important to consider a variety of social aspects before making the decision to bring a chipmunk home as a pet.

1.   Pet Chipmunks and legal considerations

For those who like the nurturing role that chipmunks offer, the exotics make for rewarding, but needy companions. If you choose to acquire a chipmunk, it becomes necessary to take a special interest in the process through which your pet reaches you. As vast as their natural range may be, not all chipmunks can be picked from the wild and raised at the individual's will.

Potential pet owners living in the United Kingdom have little cause for concern regarding the legality of owning a chipmunk. Sourced from eastern European countries, along with Japan and China, Siberian chipmunks can be purchased from any reputable pet store dealing in exotics. In recent times, some varieties of Eastern chipmunks from the North American continent have made their way to the United Kingdom, and can also be acquired with relative ease. For potential pet owners in the United States, however, the ownership of chipmunks poses many legal obstacles.

Their withdrawing nature, aversion to domestication and relative scarcity in numbers means that chipmunks receive special protection from many states across the North American continent. Some of these rules lay restrictions on the possession of certain breeds; other laws may prohibit the acquisition or ownership of a certain breed altogether. In order to protect yourself, it is essential that you understand which members of the chipmunk family are available for a domestic livelihood in your area.

Hunting or possessing several breeds of Eastern as well as Western chipmunks, such as the Durango or Cliff chipmunks, is illegal in most parts of the United States. You may want to divert your attention to other varieties, such as the yellow-tailed, red-tailed or Townsend versions of the chipmunks; be warned, however, that even these options may not be a possibility without necessary certification in some states.

The question then arises, "can I legally own a chipmunk at all in the United States?" If you are lucky enough to be residing in such states as New York, owning a chipmunk may be as simple as picking it up from your local pet store. In other states, a quick perusal of the local Wildlife laws that govern each territory reveals that authorities mostly work to protect those species of chipmunks that are native to their land. It is generally only these breeds that will have specific guidelines dictating the terms of their sale, acquisition or ownership.

The obstacles posed by local wildlife laws do not necessarily prohibit the ownership of all breeds of chipmunks; Siberian chipmunks, native to Asian countries, are shipped to the North American continent from the United Kingdom, and can be purchased and raised without any legal complications. It is best to consider Siberian chipmunks as pets in those states that may be excessively protective of their indigenous animals.

Therefore, while you still may not be able to bring home many varieties of American chipmunks, you most certainly can give a safe and happy home to one of the many healthy Siberian varieties available for sale.

If you aren't sure who to ask for the right legal information concerning the acquisition and ownership of chipmunks as pets, you can find plenty of literature on this subject on the Internet. Each state's governmental website details information on the purchase and possession of flora and fauna. Browse through the Game and Wildlife pages for the most accurate and up-to-date information.

2. Keeping pet chipmunks around children

It is probably due to their small size and deceptively pleasing appearance, along with their depiction in the media as lovable cartoon characters, that chipmunks are believed to be suitable pets for children. If you are bringing a chipmunk to a house that has children, or plan to gift one to a young child, you should take the time to consider that this may not be the wisest idea.

While it is definitely not true for all children, most younger caregivers and chipmunks may not always develop a friendly and nurturing bond. This unlikelihood can largely be attributed to the aggressive personalities of the chipmunks, and the ease with which children can become bored of carrying out responsibilities.

We have already discussed how chipmunks, as exotics, require a specific method of caregiving that addresses their food, health, habitat and emotional needs. The child will also need to put in the required bonding time needed to tame the chipmunk and make it comfortable around the young. Since the process of bonding can take days, even weeks to accomplish, a child may quickly become impatient, whereas an adult would understand the time needed to tame the pet.

Due to their aversion at being held or handled - at least initially - children may find themselves being regularly nipped at when they try to grab their chipmunks. Again, a reasonable adult, or even a child, should know that chipmunks only bite as an act of defense, but many children tend to process the bite as an act of open hostility. This may lead to the child either abandoning the pet for fear of being bitten again, or may trigger the child's anger and cause them to hurt the pet by way of payback.

If your pet chipmunks are already tame and can socialize comfortably with children, it becomes your responsibility to ensure that the rodents are handled in the right way. With a delicate frame and bone-structure, chipmunks can be easily crushed if held too tightly. While a child may squeeze the pet on their palms as a sign of affection, they may not realize the consequence of their actions. If let loose outside the cage, chipmunks often scamper around the room, requiring diligence on the part of the caregiver. If not careful, they can easily be stepped on, leading to such injuries as a broken tail, impaired foot or crushed bones.

It is not just young children, but also teenagers who are generally advised against housing chipmunks if they cannot provide the exact care the exotics need. A spacious housing facility, a steady routine that complements the chipmunk's lifestyle and a stable income are prerequisites for acquiring a chipmunk as a pet - factors that children, teenagers and students are often unable to fulfill. If the chipmunk is housed in such cramped spaces as dormitory rooms, and is left neglected during its waking hours, the chipmunk can become easily stressed, hostile and develop behavioral disorders or fall ill.

This does not mean that children and teenagers are to be completely banned from raising or handling chipmunks. It is important that you, as a responsible caregiver, educate younger members on the right ways to interact with and care for chipmunks before you consider bringing them home. Awareness of the difference between an exotic and a common household pet such as a dog or a cat can go a long way in preparing younger children to live with chipmunks.

3.   Keeping pet chipmunks around other animals

For the emotional well being of your pet, it is often advised that you house at least a pair of chipmunks of the same color pattern together, instead of raising a solitary pet. While the personalities of the chipmunks will determine their relationship with their cage mates, it also becomes important to consider the dynamics they might share with chipmunks of a different breed, or with other animals in the vicinity.

Dynamics between chipmunks with different breeds color patterns:

As a chipmunk enthusiast, you may want to house a certain variety of chipmunks of different color patterns together. In most cases, chipmunks tend to recognize only those rodents with the same coloring as their own; other chipmunks are usually regarded with suspicion and even hostility. Factors such as gender, time of the year, and number of chipmunks per group will also impact how the pets interact with each other.

As their caregiver, it is your responsibility to check whether the breeds you have acquired can coexist peacefully within the same cage. Some breeds may be more tolerant of each other, while others may seem to have problems getting along. It has been observed by many naturalists and pet owners that Agouti or Cinnamon chipmunks tend to not be compatible with White chipmunks.

Agouti and White chipmunk males are also observed to be especially aggressive towards all other males, unless the males are all siblings or have no female in the cage to compete over. As a rule of thumb, if your chipmunks do not share the same natural range, it is best to house them in separate cages.

If you must house chipmunks with different color patterns within the same cage, try to keep their numbers and genders as balanced as possible. If you have a female alpha in one group, ensure that the other group also has a female to lead them - gender differences play a significant role in dominance among chipmunk groups. Gaining strength in numbers, the color group with more members will usually turn out to be more aggressive and may even bully the other group into submission.

Dynamics between chipmunks and other animals:

If chipmunks can become temperamental towards other members of their species housed in the same cage, it is but obvious that they would treat other animals with equal hostility. Depending on the size of the other animal, its relationship with rodents, and their natural coexistence in nature, the interaction between chipmunks and every animal comes with its own unique set of dynamics.

Other rodents such as mice, guinea pigs, ferrets, rats, etc.:

When housed with, or if they come into contact with other rodents of a similar size, chipmunks tend to react with trademark hostility. Such animals as mice and guinea pigs are best caged separately from your chipmunks, as the latter may attack or kill your mice or guinea pigs. Chipmunks are also known to bully and attack the young ones of such smaller rodents, so ensure that they are kept apart.

Rats, ferrets and other large rodents are known to bully and even attack chipmunks. Placing these animals together in the same cage may cause your chipmunk stress - even with no interference from the larger rodents.

Furthermore, despite their similar size or grouping together, chipmunks still have diets that differ from the feeding needs of other rodents such as mice, rats, ferrets or guinea pigs. Housing them together may cause your chipmunks to eat food unsuitable for them, leading to choking hazards, or even illnesses from adverse reactions.

Birds:

While a larger pet bird such as a parrot may be able to fend off a chipmunk's aggressive advances, there are high possibilities that sharing a cage will result in constant fighting and injuries, possibly even death.

If you house them in the same cage as smaller birds, such as lovebirds or canaries, or let them wander into their cages, the chipmunks may harm or kill birds and their young, even destroying and eating eggs if any are around. In addition, housing birds and chipmunks together is never a good idea in terms of hygiene and sanitation.

Larger pets such as rabbits, cats and dogs:

Whether a larger pet mammal around the house, such as a dog, cat or rabbit, will get along with your chipmunk depends mostly on the personality of the former. Being bigger in size, these animals can easily injure or kill the delicate chipmunk. A rabbit's kick, in fact, is enough to put an end to a chipmunk's life.

If your larger pets are of the playful or mischievous nature, they may also resort to chasing the chipmunk around the cage, or around the house when it's let outside. This may not always be acceptable to your rodent pet. There are also plenty of instances in which chipmunks have been eaten by larger pets that either simply snuck into the cage, or hunted them down when the smaller pets wandered outside their cage. Chipmunks, on their part, simply do not enjoy being dominated by other animals and will become distressed because of it.

4.   Things to consider before bringing home chipmunks

A variety of factors come into play when determining whether a chipmunk - or two - will be suitable as a pet for you. We have already discussed, at length, the amount of considerations you are required to make as a caregiver - from understanding the legal and social implications of housing a chipmunk, to learning what caring for this furry rodent truly entails. In order to properly summarize all the prerequisites that are best fulfilled before acquiring a chipmunk, here is a checklist of questions to ask yourself:

- Can you comfortably set aside between 400 and 600 USD (260 and 400 British pounds) every month for the care and upkeep of your pet?

- Can you fulfill all the legal requisites placed by your local authorities before owning a chipmunk?

- Can you comfortably and consistently source and provide nuts, seeds, fruits, vegetables and water that is clean and of a good quality?

- Can you locate a reputed and trustworthy exotic pet care expert/veterinarian in your area for your chipmunk?

- Can you efficiently make the premises outside the cage "chipmunk-proof" before it's time to let your chipmunk outside for play and exercise?

- Can you regularly spare time once a day to spot clean the cage, and then clear time once a week for a total cage cleanup?

- Can you be patient and handle being constantly nipped - especially during the first few weeks?

- Can you devote ample time and space on a daily basis to bonding and playtime with your chipmunk for its enrichment and wellbeing?

- Can you live with a chipmunk who may develop a restless and energetic personality, or who may abhor being touched or grabbed?

- Are you comfortable with being peed or pooped on?

- Can you comfortably handle a chipmunk when it becomes temperamental and calm it down?

- Are you ready to handle sudden behavioral shifts, aggressive impulses, or antisocial phases during the winter and breeding months?

- Can you quickly spot and address any health-related issues that many crop up in your chipmunk?

- Can you provide care for your chipmunk from a responsible person in your absence? Are you comfortable with caring for a pet for at least 5, and maybe up to 12 years?

Chapter 4: Acquiring Chipmunks as pets

Chipmunks are most easily acquired in those countries where they are indigenous. In the case of neighboring countries, chipmunks can be shipped in suitable containers that require no more than ten hours of travel during the daytime hours. In addition, the possession and ownership of chipmunks is governed by strict rules and policies in such places as the United States, making it additionally challenging to find the breed of your choice.

Eastern chipmunks are the most popularly available chipmunk breed in several states across the Northern American continent, but are protected by several state governments. Some allow possession and ownership with a license, while others prohibit the sale, purchase or poaching of chipmunks from the wild.

Western chipmunks may not be as easily available for purchase, as many breeds of the western family thrive in higher altitudes and open spaces, conditions you may not be able to provide in captivity. Siberian chipmunks can also be found in the United States, due to the advancement in housing conditions over extended shipping periods. Some states such as New York allow chipmunks to be raised and bred for personal use, but require licenses and certificates if they're to be sold by vendors.

In the eastern European countries and across the United Kingdom, the most easily available breed is the Siberian chipmunk.

Potential chipmunk owners in the United Kingdom also find it relatively easier to acquire their pets than those living in the North American continent; lenient animal ownership policies and the absence of rabies has allowed interested buyers to acquire chipmunks without legal hassle. In recent times, certain breeds of Eastern chipmunks have been made available in the United Kingdom; it is however, important to remember that eastern chipmunks have a less social nature than their Siberian cousins and may not be compatible with cage mates of their own kind, let alone of a different breed.

1. Cost of buying and caring for your pet chipmunks

It is often wrongly assumed that a pet as small as a chipmunk will not require too much money to either bring home or raise. In truth, any exotic, let alone a chipmunk, can make a considerable dent in your monthly savings, by way of upkeep and maintenance. Your chipmunk will require specific living conditions, food and medical attention to thrive, making it essential for you to consider whether you can afford raising it.

Important: please check out the websites and breeders thoroughly. Be aware that there are a lot of cowboys trading on the web. The websites mentioned in this book were active at the time of printing. However, by the time you read this book, the websites might no longer be active. That, of course, is out of my control as the Internet changes rapidly.

As a potential caregiver, you will first need to invest approximately USD 500 to 1000 (around 300 to 700 British pounds) to create a set-up for your chipmunks. Depending on the number of chipmunks you plan to bring home, an average-sized cage with no extra attachments will cost you between 250 and 500 USD (150-300 British pounds.) This price excludes the inner elements that make up an ideal environment for your pet. You will have to provide furnishings and flooring elements, such as wood shavings, chippings and bark pieces, and invest in toys and other elements that help your chipmunk exercise. This phase of preparing the habitat should set you back by around 200 USD

(125 British pounds), but can also amount to a larger sum, depending on the number of elements and quality of components you add to the cage.

The next financial considerations should be made towards the food you provide your pets with. Your chipmunks, especially if brought home as babies, will need a steady diet of nutritious food and supplements. As they settle into a routine with you, you can monitor their feeding habits and adjust their feed based on their individual habits. To start with, stocking up on food for your pets will cost you at least 50 USD (30 British pounds), and will then most likely rise based on the food preferences and growth of your chipmunks.

None of the above expenses even begin to cover the healthcare your chipmunks will require, from cursory starter vaccinations to regular monthly checkups and a probable surgical procedure or two. It is only once these primary arrangements are made that you can consider the actual cost of a pet chipmunk.

The average cost of purchasing a chipmunk ranges from 100 to 150 USD (60 to 100 British pounds), depending on the source your pet is acquired from. Private breeders and fanciers are known for raising tamer chipmunks than their store-bought counterparts - but they also cost more than the latter.

Many pet chipmunks are sold by breeders and fanciers who offer to ship the pets to locations that allow the ownership of the animals. Since the United Kingdom is a popular source of reputed chipmunk breeders, your shipping fees may add up to 200 USD (120 British pounds), or even higher.

For a healthy quality of life that is neither too sparse nor too excessive for the chipmunk, you should be prepared to part with about 750 USD (500 British pounds) as an initial investment, and then budget around 150 USD (100 British pounds) every month for habitat upkeep, toys, food and healthcare.

2.   Acquiring your pet chipmunks

Although there are a variety of chipmunk species to choose from, only a few can be domesticated and raised as pets. These boundaries have been put in place by local authorities.

Buying Chipmunks from Pet Stores

The most easily available source of chipmunks for purchase is reputed and licensed pet stores in your area. Chipmunks available at these stores are often sold at a lower rate than other sources such as breeders and fanciers, often because they have been acquired in large numbers at wholesale rates. Many stores also have online portals that allow you to select and have your chipmunk shipped to your location for an extra charge.

Chipmunks acquired from pet stores may also not be as tame or friendly as those purchased from breeders and fanciers, as taming requires the caregiver to personally devote time and attention to each animal. This may not be possible for a pet storeowner to achieve on a daily basis. Lack of individual attention and personalized care may also result in the chipmunk becoming stressed and falling ill before it reaches you.

Chipmunks who are housed together in cramped quarters without individual attention also tend to hold on to their aggressive natures in order to survive. Constant scuffles with other companions may also lead to injuries, infections and possible deformities in the rodents. If your selected chipmunk has had to compete with other cage mates for space and food for a prolonged period, it may be almost impossible to completely tame them. Chipmunks who have been acquired from such environments are rarely known to domesticate or form lasting bonds with their caregivers.

If the nearest pet store is located in another town or city, and chooses to ship the chipmunk to you, the conditions of the shipping container also determine how healthy your pet will be when it arrives at your doorstep. Dark, cramped quarters with no playthings can easily traumatize a chipmunk. Unless you personally choose your pet after making an informed decision, buying a chipmunk from a pet may not always be the wisest choice in the long-term.

When you visit the pet store to select your pet, it's best to have at least a basic idea of how to differentiate between a male and female chipmunk, as well as prepare a mental checklist of signs of a healthy chipmunk. While examining the chipmunks to select a suitable candidate, here are some probable instances at the pet store that should raise red flags and cause you to reconsider your purchase:

● The dealer cannot differentiate between a male and female chipmunk,

● The dealer has no knowledge of the date of birth or breed of the chipmunks,

● Many chipmunks have been housed together in the same quarters, making them cramped,

● The chipmunk has already begun to show signs of distress at the store.

If you choose to have your chipmunk shipped or are making your purchase online, ensure that the pet store or online retailer has a return or money-back policy in place, in case you are dissatisfied with your pet. The above red flags also apply to chipmunks that are shipped to your premises. In addition, you should also be wary if:

● The shipping crates shown to you have no hiding spaces,

● The dealer makes plans to ship the chipmunks at night - despite the chipmunks being diurnal. Activity such as being transported across borders during the night hours will prevent the chipmunks from falling asleep and cause stress.

Buying Chipmunks from Breeders

They may not be as easy to find as pet stores and online retailers, but if you are keen on bringing home a healthy chipmunk, locating your nearest reputed chipmunk breeder might be a safer and wiser option. Breeders are people who raise chipmunks for sale and profit, often caring for more than one generation at a time.

Raising the chipmunks to appeal to potential caregivers forms the livelihood of breeders; they, therefore, take great pains to provide the right kind of care to the rodents - be it housing them in spacious cages, providing timely - and ample - nutritious food, and ensuring that each chipmunk receives individual attention. Breeders also house chipmunks in compatible groups, pairings and species, allowing you to pick up multiple pets with greater chances of the chipmunks getting along. Those professionals who specialize in chipmunks will often also take an interest in raising other rodent exotics, such as ferrets, chinchillas, squirrels, sugar gliders and kinkajous, to widen your options.

Due to the exhaustive effort contributed towards raising healthy and viable chipmunks, the cost of purchasing a pet from a breeder may be a little higher than the rate offered by your neighborhood pet store. What you will receive in exchange for this extra sum, however, is a chipmunk with superior breeding, a positive social disposition and relatively good health. Breeders will also be able to accurately pinpoint each variety of chipmunk out to you, and will also have records of the date of birth, breed, vaccinations, and possibly even lineage, to share with you.

Many breeders take a personal interest in their chipmunks and like to ensure that they end up in a safe and loving house. They also have hands-on experience at caring for chipmunks, and are often good sources of information on pet care. Thorough professionals at their job, breeders will be able to properly advise on the individual personality quirks of each rodent, can help you find reputed food and housing resources, and can also refer you to a trusted exotic pet expert for healthcare.

Breeders are always looking for potential caregivers for their exotics, and will place advertisements on such platforms as newspapers, community newsletters and message boards, or even on the Internet. While largely an honest and hardworking group of people, you may still encounter the odd breeder whose concerns are more monetary than emotional. They may not have put in the effort to raise tame chipmunks, or may have ignored their health and welfare, but will still quote rates that most top-quality breeders charge. It is best to make a personal visit to the breeder if you can, before you make your purchase, in order to assess the quality of care provided to the chipmunks, as well as the trustworthiness of the seller.

Buying Chipmunks from fanciers

Fanciers are often confused with breeders since they are individuals who usually advertise chipmunks for sale from their homes. The main difference between fanciers and breeders, however, is that fanciers chance upon chipmunk babies when their own pets deliver a litter that they are unable to raise themselves. Often an unexpected surprise to the owners, chipmunks acquired from fanciers may only be of a certain variety or coloring, limiting your choices.

Since fanciers are not professional breeders, they are often not required to possess any certification or licenses. This can make them challenging to locate; their information won't be found on community pet forums or with reputed veterinarians. If they do have a litter for sale, however, fanciers will advertise through local media, and can be contacted accordingly.

Rare though these pets may be, chipmunks acquired from fanciers are likely to have a more sociable and tame personality than their store-bought and professionally bred counterparts. These chipmunks are birthed and weaned in a domestic environment, and are comfortable with human touch from the start. These chipmunks also receive individual attention and care, both from their families as well as their caregivers, making them more likely to form a bond with you. Fanciers can also be reliable sources of advice and point you towards the best veterinarian, food brands and housing options for your pets.

Buying Chipmunks in the United States and United Kingdom

Even though chipmunks may be most easily available through local pet stores, it is advisable to buy such exotic pets as chipmunks from more reputed sources like breeders. Whether you live in the United States or United Kingdom, breeders are often trusted more than any other source to sell potential owners pets that have been tamed and vaccinated.

If you live in the United States, most breeders and fanciers will place advertisements for chipmunk babies for sale on such websites as:

www.exoticanimalsforsale.net / www.domesticsale.com

www.oodle.com

In the United Kingdom, chipmunks for sale can be found on websites as:

www.preloved.co.uk / www.pets4homes.co.uk

Acquiring chipmunks from the wild

In areas that form their natural habitat, chipmunks can easily be spotted at the edge of forested areas, at campsite clearings, and even in the gardens and backyards of many residential settlements. Some chipmunks may even have preferred spots for collecting and storing food that may expose them to human contact. If you chance upon a chipmunk in the wild, it is important to understand that it cannot be picked and domesticated using techniques employed for a stray dog or cat.

As exotics, chipmunks will not become domesticated upon initial human contact. It takes weeks, even months of behavioral therapy from professionally trained rehabbers to adapt chipmunks rescued from the wild into captivity. As an amateur caregiver, you may not have the resources or the patience to provide such exacting care.

Transitioning from the wild to a captive state will require the chipmunk to learn new foraging habits, adapt to a new housing environment, and accept unfamiliar behavioral patterns from strangers not usually interacted with in their natural habitat. Without the necessary education on the matter, trying to rehabilitate a chipmunk on your own may turn quickly stressful, both for you and the animal.

Wild chipmunks may also be carriers of rabies, especially if they are found in the United States, and may infect humans if they decide to bite in defense or retaliation. Furthermore, acquiring a chipmunk from the wild is strictly prohibited by several states across the United States, and is punishable by hefty fines. If found abandoned in the wild, chipmunks are either best left alone, or rushed to the nearest exotic pet center for medical attention and rehabilitation. For the purposes of purchase, it is wise to stick with reputed and reliable sources as breeders, fanciers and pet stores - these will provide you with chipmunks that have had prior exposure to human contact and will be easy to tame and bond with.

3.   Initial Checkups and Vaccinations

Regardless of the source through which you purchase your chipmunks, it is essential that they receive medical attention before they are brought home. Depending on the care provided to your chipmunk before its sale, you may need to verify that your pet has no underlying illnesses or infections. You will also have to administer a dose of initial vaccinations.

As mammals with teeth, chipmunks, in theory, have just as much likelihood to contract rabies as other animals like dogs, horses or ferrets. If infected, rabid animals host the virus in their saliva and transfer the infection to others either through bites, or scratches and wounds that have made contact with the infected saliva. The infected animals themselves become erratic in their behavior, paranoid, irritable, and even lethargic, and uncoordinated in their movements due to severe damage incurred by their nervous system, with untreated animals eventually succumbing to the infection and dying.

Technically, domesticated animals have been studied to contract rabies at a lower rate than their wild counterparts. Developed countries like the United States and the United Kingdom have managed to keep the spread of rabies among mammalian species under control through strict vaccination programs, reducing the risk of your pet being affected.

Furthermore, members of the rodent family such as mice, squirrels and chipmunks have been studied to be rarely infected with rabies. Even so, as animals with sharp teeth and an anatomy that can host the illness, it is best to have your chipmunk vaccinated against rabies either before, or as soon as you bring it home. Several areas in the United States have made it compulsory to have any mammalian pets vaccinated against rabies soon after their birth, making an appointment with the nearest veterinarian or animal health care center necessary.

Chipmunks that have been acquired from reputed breeders and fanciers are often healthy and have already been given their course of rabies vaccinations. In the event that they haven't been, your breeder or fancier will usually inform you in advance. To prevent any chance of bringing home a potential host for rabies, however, ensure that you ask your breeder or fancier for the necessary health certificates proving that your chipmunk has been vaccinated.

Other sources such as pet store vendors may or may not have their chipmunks vaccinated against rabies; the care provided to pets within a store is usually determined by the dedication of the vendor towards selling healthy pets. Chipmunks acquired from pet stores may also have sustained injuries or contracted chest or eye infections from other members in the cage that are not instantly visible. To avoid any such mishaps, it is best to make an appointment with a reputed exotic pet expert for an initial round of checkups on the day that you purchase your chipmunk.

Electronic tagging for chipmunks

Ideally, a domesticated pet should be loyal to its immediate surroundings, and not venture too far from their homes. In the case of such pets as dogs or cats, adequate training and care is usually enough to ensure that the pet does not run away. As exotics pets, however, chipmunks, though they can be tamed, cannot always be prevented from escaping their cages and out of the house through an open door or window.

Curious and independent by nature, even the tamest chipmunk will usually want to explore its immediate surroundings, and could easily become lost. Devices such as embedded microchips act as tracking equipment to help return lost and found pets to their owners. In addition, the microchips can also record such information as the breed of the animals and the vaccinations provided, helping your veterinarian monitor your pet's care more efficiently.

Electronic tags are most commonly suggested for such animals as dogs, cats, and those domestic animals that have been raised for profit, such as goats and chickens. However, electronic tagging is not restricted to certain species of animals; it is, in fact, recommended among as many domesticated mammals as possible.

Not much larger than a grain of rice, an electronic microchip is available in different models and can easily be inserted by a reputed veterinarian with a simple procedure, should you choose to have your pet electronically tagged. This procedure is also relatively painless, and will hurt your chipmunk only as much as the prick of a needle would.

Most pet stores and breeders across the United States and United Kingdom choose to have pets such as dogs and cats electronically tagged, but this requirement may vary among chipmunk breeders and vendors. As with vaccinations, it is best to check with your breeder if your pet has been tagged, as ownership details on the microchip will have to be transferred under your name and address.

Chapter 5: Housing Conditions for your Chipmunks

1.   Setting up a house for your chipmunks

Despite their seemingly small size, chipmunks require a disproportionately large enclosure in which to roam, exercise and hide at their convenience. As active animals prone to constant bursts of activity, chipmunks will require cages that are not only spacious, but also filled with plenty of accessories for their amusement.

Ideally, an adult chipmunk housed in captivity requires a cage that is at least four feet high, three feet long and two feet wide (100 x 150 x 50 cm). Another important factor to consider is the distance provided between cage wiring. A wire distance ranging between 10 and 15 millimeters is needed to help keep your chipmunks from poking their heads or slipping out, and to help keep other pets, such as dogs and cats, from reaching for chipmunks within. As an added precautionary measure, cage doors should be fitted with latches that are sturdy enough to withstand manipulation from chipmunks and other small animals.

Such dimensions rule out most small birdcages and other cages meant for guinea pigs and hamsters. Large aviary, squirrel and chinchilla cages sold at pet stores should have the measurements necessary for your chipmunk's comfort. Most commercially manufactured cages will either be made entirely out of wire, or may be sold in wood-and-wire combination variants. Either of these is suitable for your pets - a wood-bottomed cage with a detachable bottom tray would be ideal. In the event that you find narrow cages with adequate height, two cages can also be combined together to provide more room for a pair or more of chipmunks.

The cages themselves will have to be in a room that permits chipmunks to wander outside the cages without fear of injury or attack. Cages are often insufficient in terms of exercise space needed for the chipmunks. While chipmunks enjoy climbing furniture and perching on top of wardrobes and closets, a house filled with people and pets may put them at risk of being stepped over or even eaten. They may also hurt themselves on sharp furniture edges or nibble through important wiring and electrical cords. To prevent such mishaps, it is best to select an area in the house that can sustain cages and chipmunks without any interference from other family members.

Owing to the exact standards needed to comfortably house a solitary chipmunk, let alone a group of exotics, finding the ideal cage or enclosure can pose a considerable challenge. Most pet stores stock cages that are wider than they are long, and enclosures for chipmunks may need to be ordered in advance. If you find yourself facing a similar challenge, and possess basic carpentry skills, it may be more convenient - and economical - to source the necessary materials and build the cage yourself. Many independent furniture repair shops and contractors will also build you a cage that suits your requirements for 100-200 USD (65-130 GBP) within a day, if they have the time and materials.

2.   Furnishing the cage

Chipmunks housed in captivity are often exposed to unfamiliar surroundings, especially for the first few days in a new owner's house. A cage placed in the corner of the room with one side preferably facing a wall provides chipmunks with a safe and familiar corner to which they can retreat in times of stress or perceived threat.

Once a suitable cage is selected, it must be furnished in a way that is aesthetically pleasing as well as functional for the chipmunks. Padding the floor about 2-3 feet deep with materials that encourage burrowing habits and storage of food should be your first priority. You can incorporate such elements from nature as soft soil, peat and moss - beware, however, that soft earth, if used in an indoor cage, can cause a mess in its vicinity.

Pet owners also choose to pad the floor of the cage with hay and thick strips of cloth. Many pet stores also carry commercially prepared pet bedding with a variety of bases, such as coconut husk or paper, which can be used for the flooring. Refrain from using such fine substances as sawdust when filling in the floor of the cage. Pine and cedar wood are also best avoided, as they may irritate the sensitive eyes of the chipmunk. You can also place small patches of cloth that can be used at floor mats for the chipmunks to rest on.

The next essential element in the chipmunk's cage is a small, covered space within the enclosure that will be used for sleeping, storage of food and privacy. Chipmunks generally use the inner hollows of trees, logs, or burrows holes into the ground to sleep in; you will have to provide a resting space that is similarly private in nature. Nest boxes with a small hole for entry and exit are sold for aviary purposes in pet stores, and make for ideal resting, hibernating and birthing spaces for chipmunks. The inside of the nest boxes should be lined with soft materials such as newspaper wads or strips of cloth that help keep the chipmunk incubated.

Depending on the model and make of your cage, you may need to provide a separate tray under the cage floor to collect droppings, discarded food and stray flooring bits that fall from the cage. Most wire cages have no firm flooring, and can be placed on top of a tray or sheets of newspapers, which are collected and cleaned on a weekly basis. If you find cages with detachable cleaning trays, however, extra collection material may not be required.

After the basics of the cage are taken care of, other elements within the cage should all be aimed towards providing exercise, as well as ensuring that the chipmunk does not become bored. Filling their waking hours with such activities as digging, climbing, chasing cage mates and running, an absence of toys and accessories in the cage will promote emotional wellbeing and keep behavioral disorders at bay.

There is no limit - or budget - for the amount of accessories that can be added to your cage. At higher points, attach bars and perches for chipmunks to suspend themselves from. Branches from fruit trees are safe enough for chipmunks to perch and gnaw on, and also simulate the feeling of a natural environment.

At the floor level, chipmunks can entertain themselves for hours on end if provided with a small, artificially constructed network of tunnels and burrows. These tunnels can easily be crafted using sheets of cardboard and PVC glue. Cardboard sheets are just as useful for constructing play cubbies and nests in the corners of the cage for privacy. Large, smooth pebbles and rocks can also be assembled in small formations around the cage - chipmunks tend to use such spots as markers for food storage and hiding.

Finally, toys will have to be added in the cage to help alleviate boredom and keep the chipmunks active. There are no particular requisites that constitute an ideal chipmunk toy; as long as the toy can be grasped and moved, your pet will be content. Common toys found in chipmunk cages include tiny soft balls, bells and partially used rolls of toilet paper (which also help chipmunks add padding to their personal nest boxes). It may seem natural to add in a hamster-wheel, but refrain from doing so; such accessories are harmless when the chipmunk is emotionally stable, but may trigger stereotypical behavioral disorders among your pets, especially during stressful times such as breeding and hibernation.

3.   Chipmunk-proofing the room housing the cage

Your chipmunks will not restrict their movements to the confines of the cage; inquisitive and energetic by nature, they are most content when allowed to explore the entirety of their surroundings. Promoting free-range roaming is also a healthy habit that instills a sense of security in your pets, and helps them bond faster with their caregivers. Several elements in a human habitat, however, may either harm delicately built creatures like chipmunks, or they, in turn, may gnaw on prized possessions in the house.

It is a combination of the need for ample space for cages and exploring that makes empty, undisturbed rooms in the house a perfect spot to house chipmunks in. Such objects as electrical fittings and sharp furniture should be moved out of the room, along with other destructible items like books, glass items and chinaware, or favored pieces of clothing and upholstery. Windows in the room should ideally be locked firmly to prevent chipmunks from escaping out of the room.

Chipmunks are also often at risk of being stepped on by members in the house as they hurry across the floor, and they are just as likely to be eaten by larger pets on the premises. To prevent such accidents, it is best to keep the room locked at all times, save for feeding, cleaning and bonding sessions.

Rooms meant for chipmunk housing can also serve as storage areas for their personal belongings. Several chipmunk owners use an empty tool shed, garage or even the attic in their houses as a safe housing and storage area. Chests filled with feeding, cleaning and playtime supplies for the cage can be installed in this room, to help contain all chipmunk-related activity within the area.

Chapter 6: Interacting with your Chipmunks

1.   Bonding with your Pet Chipmunks

A newly acquired chipmunk, whether a young puppy or a fully-grown adult, is often suspicious of and aggressive towards a new owner. If the chipmunk has been purchased from a professional breeder or fancier, it may display lower signs of aggression, but may still withdraw from your touch and become shy in your presence. In order to help form a connection with your chipmunk, an initial period of bonding is essential, even compulsory.

The extent to which a caregiver bonds with their chipmunk largely affects the feeding habits, playtime and other instances that may force the two to interact. A healthy bond developed within the first week of the chipmunk's arrival ensures that such tasks as feeding and medical attention can be adhered to at the earliest.

In theory, a caregiver can begin to enforce a bond with the chipmunk from the second week of its birth. The puppy, however, will only be able to open its eyes completely by the fourth week, and will respond to bonding and training exercises by the seventh week of age. Most breeders will only sell chipmunks who have been completely weaned off milk and puppy milk replacer; this places the age of the chipmunk between eight and ten weeks, making the exercise of bonding an immediate necessity.

Bonding with unweaned chipmunks

Unweaned chipmunks between the ages of two and six weeks will still be new to such sensations as touch, sight and sounds. As a caregiver, you can help your pet familiarize itself with your scent. Begin by touching the young chipmunk for a minute or two for the first two days, until the chipmunk recognizes your scent and touch. When it is prepared, carry the chipmunk for a few minutes at intervals of three or four hours, until you are able to carry it in your palm without causing stress for up to 20 minutes.

You can also help your chipmunk adapt to your scent by carrying it in the front pocket of the sweatshirt you are wearing; alternatively, you can carry the chipmunk around in a large shirt pocket, or even rest with the young animal on your lap. The eventual aim is to make the chipmunk completely at ease in your presence. You can then carry on with bonding exercises used to train adult and weaned chipmunks.

Bonding with weaned chipmunks

If your chipmunks have already been weaned at the time of purchase, you may be able to bond with them simply by luring them out of their cages with the help of treats and rewards. Weaned chipmunks are independent enough to wander to recognize your scent, voice and touch without having to be held; in order to further the process of bonding, however, cradling your chipmunk for a few minutes each day may not be an unwise bonding choice.

Chipmunks, upon entering their new homes, will first retreat to their hiding spots, choosing to emerge at mealtimes. To help draw them out of their nest boxes, place a treat in the palm of your hand when you spot the chipmunk exploring the contents of the cage. Avoid making sudden movements, as it may startle the chipmunk. Such food items as berries, peanuts and other nuts are often favored over pieces of vegetables. Ensure that the treats provided are tempting enough to entice the chipmunk.

After a few suspicious sniffs, chipmunks will eventually succumb and arrive to pick the treat from the caregiver's palm. At this point, you can grasp your chipmunk gently by enclosing its body gently within your palms. If this startles the chipmunk, maintain a steady yet soft grip until the animal calms down. With time and practice, chipmunks will learn to trust the grip of your palm. Once they seem unconcerned by your fingers encasing their body, gently lift them out of the cage and allow them to explore the exercise room to their heart's content.

The rate at which your chip will develop a bond with you is largely determined by the amount of time you spend in the chipmunk's presence. The more your pet is exposed to your presence, the faster it can adapt to your role as its caregiver. Ideally, successful bonding is said to be made possible by spending at least three to four hours with the chipmunk during the first three weeks, and then maintaining an interaction of at least an hour daily.

The possibility of biting and "wilding up"

As much time and patience as it may take to build a bond of trust and care with your pet, the chipmunk can easily revert back to its "wild" state if left neglected for prolonged periods of time. Social and interactive by nature, chipmunks require constant stimulation in the form of interpersonal interactions, exercise and playtime in order to promote health and wellbeing. Chipmunks who are left in isolation or without any source of amusement can also become stressed and paranoid, and may attack its caregiver as a result.

It is important to understand that chipmunks will only ever bite as an act of defense; they are generally more shy than aggressive in the presence of humans. If your chipmunk does attempt to nip at your fingers around the late summer or autumn months, it may be doing so to protect its reserve of food burrowed within the cage. Once completely tame, many chipmunks refrain from biting their caregivers, even when undergoing periods of aggression and hostility. If your pet makes a habit of nipping or biting at you, it can easily be taught to stop such behaviors.

For every nip administered by the chipmunk, give it a firm tap on the nose or a little pinch on the back of the neck. This sudden admonishing behavior may only startle the chipmunk at first, but will discourage it from nipping at you if carried out every time the chipmunk bites.

2.   Training your Pet Chipmunks

Despite possessing a stubborn nature, chipmunks can be trained to respond to individual names, arrive when called, and can even be taught simple tricks such as somersaulting on command. The ability to successfully train the chipmunk to perform tricks is largely determined by the amount of time you can devote towards training, along with the bond you have already built with your pet. If the chipmunk is comfortable around the caregiver's presence, tricks can be picked up through simple methods such as classical conditioning.

With a limited understanding of vocabulary, chipmunks can still grasp such simple commands as "yes", "no", "come", "roll", etc. They are also sensitive to such intricacies as the inflections of vocal tones and difference in speech patterns during different moods. Their ability to decipher one motion from the next helps chipmunks understand the intent behind most of your commands, even if they may grasp the word.

The first piece of training you will provide will be teaching the chipmunk to respond to its given name. This exercise can be undertaken when you first begin bonding exercises with the chipmunk; each time you place a treat in your palm, call out to the pet using its name. Initially, the chipmunk may only arrive to take the treat from your palm; the sound you make will have little effect on its ability to arrive when called, as it does not yet have understanding of its name. If practiced for ten minutes at intervals of every hour or two, your chipmunk should learn to accept treats from your palm within a week.

Once the chipmunk begins taking the treat out of your palm each time, introduce an alternative into the exercise. Switch between calling out the pet's name and offering the treat in silence. Withdraw the treat from its grasp if its tries to take the food without being called, and reward the chipmunk each time it responds successfully to its name. With a few tries, which may take up to a week to accomplish, your chipmunk will understand the importance of its name as an identifier, and will respond to your call even in the absence of a treat.

Once the chipmunk grasps such concepts as responding to its name, use this method to teach it other behaviors, such as climbing, chasing a toy or somersaulting on command. With time and practice, your pet will not only learn the commands you teach it, but will also look forward to receiving such instructions as part of its play time.

3.   Playtime and Exercise

Bonding and training exercises can help you build a relationship of trust with your chipmunk, but these interactions do not constitute playtime for your chipmunk. Energetic by nature, chipmunks will use up about half of their waking hours indulging in some form of exercise and play in the wild; in captivity, it becomes your responsibility to facilitate this.

To maintain optimum health, an adult chipmunk requires at least an hour of active exercise each day, provided through such activities as climbing, running, swinging from perches and burrowing. Most chipmunks do not require any form of encouragement during play and exercise times; they will either play amongst themselves or explore outer surroundings as part of their exercise routine.

This is why it becomes essential for you to provide your chipmunks with a chipmunk-proof room that they can explore at ease. Such items within the room as curtain rods, shelves and empty bookcases help add intensity to the exercise received by the chipmunks.

Within the cage, chipmunks housed in groups will most often chase each other or collect and hide away food as part of their exercise. For further stimulation, such toys as small balls, bells, bowls, and swings can be added. Many owners may also add a rodent wheel into the cage, as chipmunks can receive ample exercise from running around the wheel in circles. In times of stress, however, chipmunks tend to take to running constant circles on the wheel due to stereotypical behavioral disorders. The addition of a rodent wheel, therefore, must be carefully considered.

4. Understanding interactions between chipmunks in the group

As a caregiver, you may choose to attempt raising a group of chipmunks from the start, or may decide to bring home a companion for your solitary chipmunk at a later stage. Regardless of the timing of your decision, housing more than one chipmunk impacts the personality that your pets will grow up to display, and will also impact their relationship with you as a caregiver. In order to better understand how to interact with your pets, it becomes equally important to pay attention to relationships that your pets share with each other.

Chipmunks of the same sex tend to become instant friends when introduced to a new cage at the same time. It becomes additionally easy for your chipmunks to bond, whether male or female, if they are introduced to each other between the ages of six and eight weeks. It is during this developmental period that most chipmunks form social bonds; any companions within the cage will be greeted with enthusiasm.

Gender differences generally do not affect the relationship between two offsprings. A male and female chipmunk, if housed together, will get along just as well as same-sex exotics raised in the same cage. Most pet owners refrain from housing a male and female sibling pair without the addition of other unrelated companions. In the absence of unrelated chipmunks, siblings may turn towards each other during the breeding season, and may even produce a litter. Such a situation is best avoided, as the resulting litter often contains babies with deformities, weak immune systems and behavioral disorders.

If you have brought home an entire family of chipmunks, you will have to make provisions to accommodate the evolving relationship between parents and their offspring. Upon birth, mothers are extremely protective of their chipmunks, and assume feeding and weaning responsibilities until the puppies are around eight weeks old. From this point, the now-adolescent chipmunks are expected to fend for themselves, and regarded by others in the cage as adults. Mothers and daughters are often compatible long after the weaning period is over; fathers and sons, on the other hand, can only be housed together with the families until the sons attain sexual maturity at ten months. After this point, fathers will compete with their sons for female attention, resulting in fights and injuries.

Chipmunks and the tendency to fight

While largely sociable by nature, chipmunks raised in captivity may also be prone to aggressive outbursts on occasion, or may display a hostile attitude towards certain cage mates during particular times. During the summer months, most chipmunks will display signs of sociability and friendliness towards other chipmunks; aggressive tendencies are often a personal trait not shared by all exotics raised in captivity. At the onset of the winter season, however, chipmunks seem to undergo a transformation in personality, becoming hostile towards their cage mates, and picking fights at every given opportunity.

With an innately territorial disposition, most chipmunks tend to be highly protective of their personal nesting and storage spaces. Any perceived threat to their space, whether from a new or existing cage mate, will be met with suspicion, even hostility.

If your chipmunk has been raised in isolation, a new cage mate may not always be greeted positively. The newer pet may find itself being bullied by the older cage member, and may become stressed as a result. Chipmunks are also as relentless as they are aggressive, and are unlikely to stop pursuing their victims unless the latter is removed from the cage. If the new cage member is just as resilient as the older chipmunk, however, a series of fights to determine dominance may ensue, and will have to be stopped before the animals are injured.

It is not always easy to distinguish between fighting and playtime behaviors among chipmunks. Chipmunks enjoy spending their spare time chasing each other around the cage; if they share a good relationship, the casing will end with each chipmunk going to their individual nest boxes. When a chipmunk pursues their victim with the intent of bullying, however, they do not stop until the victim has been pinned down on its back.

If the victim chipmunk finds itself on its back under a dominant chipmunk, it may succumb to a series of injuries inflicted by the bully in the form of nips and scratches across the nose, ears and eyes. If the chipmunk decides to fight back, it will push against the weight of the bully, resulting in the chipmunks tumbling across the cage in a violent, furry ball. It may be difficult to physically separate chipmunks once they entangle themselves in a hostile ball; a toy water pistol used in effective bursts has proven ideal at startling chipmunks and sending them scurrying to their nest boxes.

If the older chipmunk does not adjust to the presence of the new cage mate, it is best to separate the two pets and house them in individual cages. Chipmunks who have been bullied by other members of their species, if left unattended, withdraw into their nest boxes, refusing to emerge even when hungry. They may also choose to forage for food when the bully is asleep and become nocturnal as a result. In order to avoid putting the chipmunk under such stress, immediate separation and rehabilitation is essential.

Introducing an old chipmunk to a new cage mate

Despite your best intentions, you may not always be able to provide a separate space for a new chipmunk who is being bullied within the same premises, In other cases, you may intend for the new chipmunk to get along with the older cage mate for the purpose of breeding. If such situations arise and bring about the need to house a new chipmunk within the same cage, there are several precautionary measures you can take to ensure that your pets' exposure to each other is gradual and measured.

Before you bring home a new chipmunk, it is best to enclose it within a smaller cage stocked with food, bedding and a nest box. For the first two weeks, the new chipmunk will stick to the space within its cage, and may wander towards the edges to peek at the outer cage. The older chipmunk, on its part, will sniff at the contents of the inner cage, becoming curious of the environment within. Allow the chipmunks to familiarize themselves in this setting in each other's presence, until you notice them gathering along the cage to sniff at each other.

After a period of two weeks, place the new chipmunk in the larger cage, while housing the older chipmunk in the newer, smaller cage. This isolated time in each other's environments allows the pets not only to familiarize themselves with the new habitat, but also with each other's scent and sounds. Upon switching houses, chipmunks will usually break the ice and interact with each other by touching their nose through gaps in the wiring. If the chipmunks show a persistent interest in each other for over two weeks, you can then remove the smaller cage from the environment, and let the chipmunks directly interact with each other.

This period of shared rehabilitation often helps new cage mates view each other in a positive light, leading to a peaceful coexistence. If this exercise of shared rehabilitation has been unsuccessful, chipmunks may begin fighting within minutes of being introduced to each other. Should this possibility occur, it is best to separate the chipmunks and consider raising them individually until they are ready to breed.

Chapter 7: Pet Chipmunks and Feeding Habits

1.   What to feed your chipmunks

Fruits

Fruits are some of the most favored foods of the chipmunk species, and you can incorporate a variety of fresh fruit to provide nutrition. Popular fruits include grapes, blackberries, kiwis, pineapple pieces, strawberries, melon cubes and raspberries. Some fruits will need to be prepared before feeding to the chipmunk in order to avoid choking hazards or unnecessary illnesses.

Bananas should preferably be peeled and chopped up before serving. Apples and oranges are prized foods, but will need to be de-piped in advance. The stones should be removed from such fruits as peaches, cherries, plums, nectarines and mangoes. The seeds of nectarines, avocados and mangoes, and the skin of avocados in particular, have been studied to be poisonous and cause toxicity in the chipmunks' systems. Apple pips have also been found to be poisonous to some extent. Exceptions are those seeds from some fruits, such as melon, watermelon, pumpkin and pomegranate, which have not been found to cause toxicity, and can be left in the flesh.

Vegetables

Chipmunks may not show the same enthusiasm towards all vegetables as they do for fruit. Roots, leafy greens and other vegetables they do show a preference for tend to be on the sweeter side, displaying their preference for food with a sugary element.

Among the accepted vegetables are peas, sprouts, carrots, chicory, cauliflower, endives, kale and sweet corn kernels shaved off the cob. Vegetables can be provided raw, but should preferably be chopped into bite-size cubes. Accepting a large portion of vegetables into their diet will often depend on the personality and taste preferences of each individual chipmunk, so it is best to try out a number of vegetables with your pets to ascertain their palate.

You can also introduce such produce as lettuce and cabbage leaves, along with a few cubes of cucumber. This trio of foods should preferably not be mixed in the same meal, and should also be provided sparingly. While your pets may develop a taste for cucumbers, lettuce and cabbage leaves, the chemical composition of these foods in excess can cause an upset stomach.

Nuts

As you may have guessed, chipmunks will be most excited about the nuts you have to offer them; the larger the variety, the happier your pets will be. Whether picked freshly from the ground, picked up by the bag from a vendor, or scooped out from a frozen stash of pet food, chipmunks will accept nuts in almost any shape or form. Most nuts can and should be handed over to the chipmunks in their shell. While being easy enough and a fun task to crack open, this activity also gives your pets the opportunity to trim their teeth against the hard surfaces of the shells.

Peanuts are the most favored member of the nut family, and will likely be gobbled up greedily. Other nuts you can feed your pet chipmunks include almonds, walnuts, hazelnuts, pecans, pine nuts, monkey nuts, sweet chestnuts, macadamia nuts, and hickory nuts. Brazil nuts can also be fed; however, these nuts have a tougher shell than others and can be tough for your chipmunk to crack. You may need to make the first dent or chip in the shell for your pet.

If you can find acorns in your area, freshly fallen ones make for great chipmunk treats. When you do pick your acorns, try to collect those that have either just fallen or are hanging loose from trees; old acorns will likely have become moist and may already have begun to decay. If you must, acorns can also be frozen in large quantities and defrosted before feeding your pets.

Flowers, Seeds and Grains

As creatures who usually forage in the wild for food, chipmunks will also easy the flowers, seeds, grains and plants that agree with their digestive systems and please their palate. If available in your area, chipmunks will contentedly munch on rose hips and rose petals, wild daisies, marigolds, clover, hibiscus, magnolia, honeysuckle and hawthorn. While these flowers are acceptable, not all plants and flowers can be digested by a chipmunk; some may cause severe toxicity. It is best to check with your local exotic pet expert if the plants available to you are suitable for your pet. Grains and seeds that can be added to your chipmunk's feed include wheat, oats and sunflower seeds.

Live feed

They may largely be content with vegetarian sources of food such as nuts, seeds fruits and vegetables, but the chipmunks' omnivorous nature means that your pets will consume meat with equal gusto. Live feed in the form of small bugs and insects is also essential to help maintain healthy levels of calcium, phosphorus, proteins and vitamins. This is why you may find the remains of the odd cricket or spider that wandered into the chipmunks' cage.

Live feed sources that are both comfortable for you to handle and accepted by the chipmunks include mealworms and crickets, available at bait and pet stores in fresh and dried form. Hard-boiled eggs chopped into small pieces are also good sources of protein for your chipmunks. You can also feed small cubes of chicken, fish, beef and ham to your pets, but it is best that the meat is cooked beforehand and provided sparingly, about once a week.

Other acceptable foods

As omnivorous mammals, chipmunks possess a palate and digestive system that is open to sampling a diverse array of foods. From fruits and nuts to cooked meats, the daily diet of chipmunks consists of items that can easily be sourced from your personal food supply, rarely leaving you without option during the pet's' feeding time.

In fact, you will find that your pet chipmunks, in addition to eating most foods available from your pantry, will also curiously peck at any stray food items they may come across during playtime. With a love for sugary and crispy substances, many pet owners have noticed their chipmunks developing a taste for cookies and biscuits, certain varieties of chips and other snacks. Depending on the taste preferences of your pets, and the nutritional value of the snack itself, you can choose what human foods to introduce to your chipmunks' diet.

Foods from your snack cupboard that will likely be accepted by your chipmunk include biscuits, wafers, pretzels, crackers, potato and corn crisps, wheat, puffed rice and corn cereals among others. Chipmunks enjoy a sweet flavor in their foods, and lap up such spreads as peanut butter, honey, and fresh fruit jam. A small serving of peanut butter or honey, given about once in ten days as a treat, will delight your pet. Making foods such as sugary biscuits and peanut butter available on a daily basis, on the other hand, is not advisable.

2.   Dry food mixes and muesli for chipmunks

Owing in part to the varied omnivorous nature of the chipmunk's diet, it has been relatively difficult to properly isolate a diet that provides the perfect nutritional requirements for your pet. Most food that you will provide will comprise of fresh fruit and vegetables, along with individual servings of nuts and seeds with varying degrees of nutritional value. To help ensure a consistent and regulated source of essential vitamins and minerals, you can rely on reputed, commercially prepared dry food mixes.

Also known as chipmunk muesli, these mixes are available from such brand names Pets at Home, Beaphar Xtra Vital, Johnson and Jeff Chipmunk and Squirrel mix and Burgess Supa Chipmunk mix. Each brand formulates its own composition and variety of nuts, seeds, grains, dried fruit, and formulated chipmunk biscuits, and are usually available in bags weighing up to 1 kilogram (about ½ a pound). What brand you settle with will eventually depend on your chipmunks' taste buds; different pets have been known to have individual taste preferences.

Each brand will also supplement its feed with vitamins and minerals differently. Pets At Home, for example, does not enhance their mix with calcium, unlike other brands. Other brands may have generalized mixes for such pets as squirrels, chipmunks and hamsters. Make your purchase based on the contents of the mix - what your chipmunks like to eat, and how much nutritional value each brand can add to your provided food.

Dry food mixes and chipmunk bread are easy to find and purchase, whether in the United States or in the United Kingdom. Most pet stores carry brands such as Xtra Vital and Burgess Supa Chipmunk mix. Pets At Home is a brand with several outlets peppered across the United Kingdom for you to visit. In the absence of a physical location, chipmunk mixes can just as easily be ordered through pet service retail websites on the Internet.

Preparing Chipmunk Muesli at home

Upon simple inspection, you will find that commercially prepared chipmunk feed, for the most part, contains a mixture of nuts, seeds and grains that you can be easily sourced from local markets. These feeds are then supplemented with nutritionally enriched biscuits, and enhanced with essential vitamins such as A, D and E, and minerals like calcium, zinc and magnesium. If you do not have the time or resources to purchase commercially manufactured feed for your pet, take about thirty minutes to prepare your own Chipmunk muesli with the following components:

- about half the contents of the muesli should have a nut-content, from such items as walnuts, almonds, pine nuts, monkey nuts and peanuts.

- the other thirty percent should comprise of grains and seeds such as oat, wheat and sunflower seeds.

- devote ten percent to such dried items as corn kernels and dried apricots, prunes and raisins.

- the final ten percent can comprise of either commercially prepared chipmunk or squirrel biscuits, available at most pet supply stores in bulk packets, or chipmunk bread (also found at supply stores). You can also incorporate both elements into the feed in equal parts.

- store the mixture in dry, airtight containers in a cool, dark and dry place and check for freshness every week. The mix, if kept sealed after each use, should last for three to six months, depending on the contents.

3.   Nutritional intake and supplements

Chipmunks do not generally follow a restrained diet and can derive nutritional value from nearly all food sources they consume. Most of your chipmunks' feed, however, will largely comprise of food sources that provide healthy fats, vitamins, and a varying degree of minerals. If you supply commercially prepared food to your pets, depending on the brand, your chipmunk may not receive the adequate amount of minerals such as protein, calcium and phosphorus essential for bone development and health.

To help impart a healthy dose of calcium and phosphorus into the chipmunks' diet, add in a cube of cheese to each feed, along with a spoonful of yogurt provided every two to three days. Vitamin D, most abundantly available through sunlight, is also needed for bone growth, and can be provided by adding fresh mushrooms to the feed. You will also find vitamin supplement powders for chipmunks that can be added to the pet's' drinking water or fruit juice about once a week to supplement vitamin reserves.

Apart from ensuring that the chipmunks' nutritional needs are met, it is also essential that these minerals be provided in the right proportions. You may add in extra calcium supplement powder, thinking it healthy for your pets, but an imbalance could easily turn lethal. Essentially, your chipmunks' daily feed should consist of food sources that provide calcium and phosphorus in a 2:1 ratio. It is crucial that your chipmunk receive more calcium than phosphorus in its diet; excess phosphorus leads the body to throw away calcium. A resulting deficit of calcium will cause the animal's body to extract the mineral from its bones, weakening your pet and causing Metabolic Bone Disease. In addition, excess calcium without phosphorus added could lead to bone irregularities and other defects.

While it may be challenging for you to ascertain the ideal mineral and vitamin intake for your pet, your chipmunks, on the other hand, can instinctively feel a deficiency of essential vitamins and minerals. To repair this deficit, they will look for food sources rich in minerals, feeding off it until their systems are replenished. A convenient means of providing mineral and vitamin supplements is by placing commercially prepared mineral blocks and cuttlefish bones outside the pet's cage.

Mineral blocks, also known as chipmunk bread, are nutritionally dense food blocks prepared specifically to fulfill a chipmunk's dietary needs. They can be suspended by a strong piece of twine outside the cage, and left for the chipmunk to use. After an initial sniff-and-taste, your pets will know to return to the block when they experience a dip in nutritional balance. A popular, trusted type of mineral blocks for chipmunks is the VitaKraft Vita Fit Mineral Block, accepted by most chipmunks, and easily available at most pet stores and online retailers. You can also find flavored or fruity variations of these blocks, if your pets develop a taste for them.

Cuttlefish bones are another excellent source of calcium, and one that can be consumed at the chipmunks' convenience. Hung alongside the mineral blocks or simply placed on the floor of the cage, your pets will gnaw at the bone if they need a calcium boost. As a dietary precaution, you can also use finely powdered cuttlefish bones and sprinkle them over the chipmunks' feed about once a week.

If you find that your pets have left the mineral blocks and cuttlefish bones untouched, this is usually a good sign that the feed you prepare is nutritionally complete. Do not remove the blocks and bones simply because they aren't being used; your pets will be drawn to them when and if the need arises.

4.   Composition and Frequency of the feed

An adult chipmunk will require about 28 to 30 grams of food a day, which it will collect, feed on and store for future use. As it is part of their nature, chipmunks like to forage for their feed and will prefer collecting it for themselves. A ceramic bowl placed in a sturdy corner of the cage can easily act as a forage point, and saves you from making repeated trips to the cage at feeding times.

Around half of the contents of this feeding bowl should comprise seeds and nuts, which are primary food sources for most chipmunks. Another thirty percent of the feed should ideally contain a variety of acceptable fruits and vegetables, with the remaining fifteen percent devoted to commercially available chipmunk food-mixes and muesli. For a healthy intestinal gut that keeps the animal's probiotic levels intact, you should also feed your pet a teaspoon of yogurt once every two or three days. This spoonful can either be placed in the feeding bowl if your chipmunk likes the taste, or mixed with a small serving of fruit juice.

Since chipmunks are omnivorous by nature, live feed such as snails, mealworms and small bugs are not only accepted, but are also essential as part of their diet. A small mealworm or snail provided once or twice a week would help fill up their non-vegetarian diet requirement. Many pet owners have observed that refilling the feeding bowl once every alternate day encourages the chipmunk to eat all items, whether immediately or at a later time. Instead of relying on fixed routines to replenish the feeding bowl, take some time to observe your chipmunks' feeding habits to assess the frequency of the feed.

Most chipmunks will not eat all the food placed in the feeding bowl. Polishing off those items that may rot and decay, such as live feed, fruit or vegetable pieces, they tend to collect foods like nuts and seeds in their cheek pouches and hide them in secure spots within the cage. Rather than an act of collecting food to prevent starvation, this is simply a survival instinct that kicks in on a daily basis within your pets. If you provide a constantly replenished bowl, your pets may develop picky food habits, and become defensive of their vast food storage reserves.

Chipmunks tend to feed less in the winter months, especially if you encourage hibernation and torpor. During this time of year, between 20 and 25 grams of food should help your pets thrive. Aged chipmunks have also been observed to require less food than those at their adult prime; you can modify the quantity and frequency of the feed by studying their habits.

Before the winter months, however, whether or not you encourage hibernation, your chipmunks will begin a frenzied collecting and storing of nuts and seeds by way of preparation. If you allow them to hibernate, provide about 5-10 grams of extra food, with nuts and seeds making up most of the added content. Female chipmunks that are pregnant and nursing will also need extra feed to provide the extra nourishment.

Baby chipmunks, on the other hand, cannot be fed solid foods right after birth, especially if they are not nursed by their mothers. They will need to be fed commercially prepared puppy formula that provides for their nutritional needs for the five weeks. From this point, you, as a caregiver, will gradually introduce solid foods into their environment and wean them off the formula.

5.   Water for your chipmunks

Clean drinking water should be constantly available for the chipmunks at a safe distance from the food bowl and away from the bottom of the cage. You should avoid supplying water through a deep dish or bowl, as their tiny size and the possible flimsy nature of the dish may topple them into the water. Additionally, elements from the cage such as the bedding or a play area may become damp and wet, while the quick scampering nature of the rodents could also make the water dirty and unfit for drinking.

Ideally, water bottles for chipmunks should have a tiny mouth and are best hung on the wire mesh at high points outside the cage - water bottles manufactured especially for hamsters, rabbits and birds fulfill these requisites. The feeders should be replenished with fresh drinking water on a daily basis (sometimes several times a day, as chipmunks drink copious amounts of water), and placed away from direct sunlight to avoid a buildup of algae on the plastic surfaces. Placing the bottle in sunnier parts of the cage (while keeping the feeder in a shaded area) also helps your chipmunk receive its daily supply of Vitamin D, essential for calcium absorption and bone development.

Water-feeders are very slim in build and can be cleaned comfortably with soft bottlebrushes and some warm water on a weekly basis. If you house a large group of chipmunks, it is also wise to sterilize the bottles for a few minutes in boiling water. This weekly cleanup helps to prevent algae buildup and keeps the feeders disinfected and safe from possible infections.

During the winter months, in areas with freezing conditions and snowfall, the water within the feeders may freeze up, especially if the cage is housed outdoors. In such cases, the water within the bottle can be defrosted with a tablespoon of hot water, or can be left to melt naturally while you replace the frozen feeder with another bottle.

6.   What not to feed your chipmunks

Chipmunks are among the easier members of the exotics family to feed; they have an inquisitive palate and can stomach most foods commonly available to humans. Natural food sources such as nuts, fruits and vegetables, when given in adequate portions, can enrich your chipmunk's health. Processed and pre-packaged foods prepared for human use, however, though loved by the chipmunks, can be harmful for their health.

Many processed foods are often laden with levels of fat, sugar and sodium high enough to alarm even the most indulgent humans. When fed to tiny creatures like chipmunks, the adverse effects of excess sodium, sugar and fats are amplified, quickly becoming lethal. Such food items as chips, biscuits, deep fried snacks such as French fries or cheese sticks, and other junk food items should preferably be kept away from the chipmunk. Certain cookies and biscuits, such as Digestive biscuits, have lower sugar content than other varieties, and can be provided in small quantities.

As a rule of thumb, all foods that could cause such ailments in the human body as high blood pressure, increased cholesterol levels and cardiac lapses will have the same effect on chipmunks, with exaggerated intensity. If your pet does develop a taste for snack items that may be potentially unhealthy, limit the role of these foods to treats handed out once a week.

Chocolate is as poisonous to a chipmunk's system as it is to a dog or cat's. It is best to avoid letting your chipmunk come into contact with any chocolate on the premises; a single taste could turn into an unhealthy addiction.

Chipmunks also enjoy the taste of a number of flowers, such as marigolds and daisies, but cannot digest all flower varieties. Two flowers in particular - buttercups and daffodils - are known to be extremely poisonous when ingested by chipmunks, and should be kept away from them. It is best to consult with your local pet expert to receive a comprehensive list of plants that are toxic to chipmunks.

Chapter 8: Caring for your Pet Chipmunks

1. Cleaning and Maintaining the Cage

You may spend large sums of money in providing the best housing conditions for your chipmunks, but if you cannot provide the time and commitment required to clean and maintain the environment, you expose your chipmunks to a variety of possible infections, ailments and emotional duress. Proper hygiene can be maintained within the cage in the following ways:

1) A daily inspection and cleaning of the cage is essential; chipmunks will deposit fecal matter, discarded food particles and lost flooring and bedding material through the wire flooring into the tray underneath.

2) The water-feeders should be cleaned with soapy water and a bottlebrush once or twice a week, and disinfected once a month.

3) The chipmunks should be left to wander around the exercise room until the cleaning and disinfecting process is complete, in order to prevent them from contracting allergies or infections from old particles.

4) The cage should be wiped clean, emptied of all elements, and then be sterilized with the help of a rodent-safe disinfectant.

5) Clean and wipe all the accessories and toys from the cage, disinfecting those as necessary.

6) Before you transfer the chipmunks back into the cage, replace all old bedding with fresh materials and rearrange items within the cage to alleviate boredom.

7) The floor bedding will have to be changed every two to three weeks. This is important, as the old bedding will, at some point, have no more room for moisture absorption. It may also have become too dirty and cannot be kept in the cage without the risk of contaminating the environment.

8) While changing the bedding, set aside nut storages buried by your pet and replace them within the new flooring to the best

of your abilities. You can also leave the food pile in the nest box.

9) A good way of telling that it is time to change your substrate is when the tank begins emitting a faint, yet horrid odor. If left unattended, this damp smell may become more intense, signaling the rotting and decomposing of your substrate.

10) Along with the flooring, the contents of the nest box should also be changed and disinfected, before placing back into the enclosure.

2. Hibernation and Care during the winter months

The winter months are a crucial time in the life cycle of a chipmunk. In the wild, most chipmunks survive the winter season by building a network of burrows and tunnels directly under the earth's surface and entering a state of torpor. As a caregiver, therefore, you will have to make special provisions to help your pets survive the winter months, particularly if you live in areas that experience bitter winters (such as parts of the United States and Canada).

In warmer climates, however, chipmunks in captivity can also be discouraged from the state of hibernation, provided factors such as sufficient incubation and food for all the cage mates is ensured. Depending on the care they can offer and their geographical location, professional chipmunk breeders and pet owners make individual decisions on whether or not hibernation in captivity is a wise decision.

In theory, the anatomy of a chipmunk is innately tuned to prepare for, and enter, a state of torpor during the winter months. When raised in captivity, however, the prolonged period of absence from the owner may undo some of the emotional bonding achieved through daily interactions and playtime. If your chipmunk shares a close relationship with the owner, however, the hibernation phase may make little difference to your long-term bond.

Whether your chipmunks are housed outdoors or raised inside your home also impacts their personal decision to enter hibernation, and determines the time spent in this state. Furthermore, a suitable environment for hibernation (with features such as complete darkness and the warm heat of the soil) can be tricky to successfully replicate in a caged environment. You will also need to monitor your chipmunks every few days, without disturbing their state of rest. Any deviation from the routine of torpor may only serve to stress your chipmunk out through the winter months instead of helping it thrive.

The decision to permit hibernation among your pet chipmunks, therefore, is a personal choice that you will have to make after careful consideration and planning. If you can set up an environment that is favorable for hibernation, the winter months could be a time of respite not only for the chipmunks, but for you as well.

Setting the cage up for hibernation

An outdoor cage may expose the chipmunks to periods of light during the day, and is unadvisable for hibernation. Prepare in advance by isolating a room on your premises - such as an empty bedroom, tool shed or garage - that can be left undisturbed by members in your house during winter.

Outdoor cages will need to be made torpor-friendly, by ensuring that each chipmunk's nest box has sufficient padding for incubation. This can be achieved by lining each nest box with extra layers of hay, or pieces of old ripped cloth. Cotton is often suggested as a suitable padding material, but may be chewed and choked on, and is best avoided.

If edifices in your area are prone to icicle and frost formation, every nest box will have to be made frost-proof, easily achieved by covering up ventilation ducts in the nest boxes with pieces of door-seal weather stripping. It is of utmost importance that your chipmunks are kept warm in winter; easily susceptible to frostbite, nipped toes and hypothermia, inadequate incubation could lead to distressing living conditions.

In the wild, chipmunks prepare for the winter months by storing large reserves of nuts, berries and seeds. In captivity, it is the food provided to them that will form their winter supply. If the cage houses a group of chipmunks together, around 10 grams of extra food per chipmunk should be provided for storage and collection in the months leading up to winter. This will help prevent unnecessary fights over a limited quantity of food.

A healthy weight among all chipmunks is as important as ensuring the right hibernation conditions. Your chipmunks will need excess fat stored in their bodies to sustain the less-active, but more energy-consuming torpor state. This is why chipmunk puppies in captivity (especially those born in the late summer or early autumn months) are often discouraged from entering hibernation in their first year of birth. A diet filled with healthy, fat-laden nuts and seeds provided in the month leading to hibernation can help bring adult chipmunks up to an ideal torpor weight.

Pet Chipmunks and common Hibernation behaviors

If preparatory conditions are favorable, chipmunks in captivity will enter a state of hibernation in October, and will only emerge as late as March the following year. During this time, chipmunks are content to live within their nest boxes, spending their hours sleeping and reaching for food stored close by for nutrition. If the winter season experiences warmer days among the cold ones, chipmunks may emerge for brief periods of exercise and social activity.

If your chipmunks have been raised in an indoor environment, or your geographical location does not witness a drastic dip in temperatures in the winter months, long periods of hibernation may be rare, or may even be replaced with brief spells of torpor once or twice a week. Torpor is nothing but a phase during which the animal goes into a deep slumber-like state. If you are new to the experience of torpor in animals, observing your chipmunk enter this state for the first time may be unnerving - some amateur owners mistake chipmunks in torpor to have dropped dead without reason. For clarity, torpor can be determined through the following indicators:

- Lowered rate of breathing,

- Lowered rate of heartbeats per minute,

- Lowered body temperature

Chipmunks housed in captivity are just as sensitive to changes in temperature as their counterparts in the wild, and will feel the need to shut down during cold spells, even if temporarily. Should your chipmunks enter a state of torpor, it is best to let them complete their rest period, and wait for them to rouse themselves. Since torpor is a state of extended rest, chipmunks may initially seem disoriented when they awaken, and may not yet have completely opened their eyes. As their bodies adjust to the waking state, chipmunks become more alert, resume control of their movements and return to their regular daily schedules.

Waking Chipmunks from a state of Torpor

It is often not advised that caregivers attempt to end the torpor state on behalf of the chipmunks - this act may disrupt the natural rhythm determined by your pet's body and cause disorientation. In some cases, such as when a chipmunk displays signs of ill health, or needs to given medical attention, it may be necessary to wake the animal from its resting state.

If you must, rousing the chipmunk can easily be accomplished by providing an adequate source of warmth. Popular methods used to rouse a sleeping chipmunk include cradling the animals in your hands for a few minutes, or exposing them briefly to a source of heat from a distance, such as a fireplace, and then placing them in a warm environment until they awaken completely.

3. Essential Chipmunk Shopping List

The following list comprises all the items you will need to care for your chipmunk on a daily basis - from housing to diet, including toys and healthcare items. Most of these products will be available at your local pet stores, whether in the United States, Canada or the United Kingdom.

Several companies also offer pet accessories for sale through online retail websites. In the United States and Canada, you can access PetSmart to find items that address your chipmunk care needs, while Pets at Home offers the same services in the United Kingdom.

Housing

Cage, preferably chipmunk cage or large aviary (indoor or outdoor)

Water feeder (1 per pair)

Feeding bowl (1-4, depending on the size of the cage and number of chipmunks)

Pet-bedding (such as Burgess or ProRep)

Feeding hay for bedding (such as Timothy)

Nest box (1 per chipmunk)

Toys and Accessories

Cage swings

Hiding cubbies

Chew toys

Soft balls (with and without embedded bells)

Toy bowls and buckets and bells

Rodent wheel (optional)

Travel carrier (such as Ferplast)

Diet

Fruit and Vegetables

Avocados	Kiwis
Apples	Mangoes
Bananas	Muskmelon
Bell pepper	Nectarines
Blackberries	Oranges
Broccoli	Papaya
Cabbage	Peas
Carrot	Peaches
Cauliflower	Pears
Cherries	Pineapple
Chicory	Plums
Cranberries	Pomegranates
Cucumber	Raspberries
Endives	Spinach
Figs	Sprouts
Grapes	Strawberries
Honeydew melon	Sweet Potato
Kale	Watermelon

Nuts, Grains, Dried fruit and Seeds

Almonds	Peanuts
Acorns	Pecan

Brazil nuts

Chestnuts

Hazelnuts

Hickory nuts

Macadamia nuts

Monkey nuts

Oats

Pine nuts

Prunes

Raisins

Sesame seeds

Sunflower seeds

Walnuts

Wheat

Flowers and plants

Clover

Daisies

Dandelions

Hawthorne

Hibiscus

Honeysuckle

Rosehips, petals

Magnolia

Marigold

Live feed

Beef

Chicken

Crickets

Fish

Ham

Mealworms

Nutritional supplements

Chipmunk muesli

Cuttlefish bones

Miscellaneous food items

Biscuits

Bread, brown or whole-grain

Prepackaged cereal mix

Cheese

Eggs, scrambled or boiled

Honey

Peanut butter

Rusks

Yoghurt

Healthcare

Mineral Block (such as Wheely)

Probiotic supplements (such as ProC)

Skin cream (such as Skin-Eze)

Vitamin Drops (such as Vetark Broad Spectrum)

Colloidal Silver

Esbilac puppy milk replacer

Nutrobal

Baytril

Rescue Remedy

Syringes, 1cc

Chapter 9: Breeding Chipmunks in captivity

The decision to breed chipmunks, whether for personal interest or profit, is not one that should be made lightly. The care of adult chipmunks alone requires great amounts of patience, commitment and attention to detail on the part of the caregiver. If undertaken with enthusiasm and with the same dedication that is provided towards the care of adult chipmunks, potential breeders will find the process of mating and breeding not only interesting, but also rewarding.

Several factors determine how successful the incoming breeding season will be for you as a potential chipmunk puppy rearer. Chipmunks mate during the late summer or winter months, with litters being delivered between April and June, or September and November. Depending on your geographic location and the climatic conditions provided, your female chipmunk may become pregnant and give birth during both breeding seasons.

The ability to successfully breed with cage mates is also impacted by the relationship of the chipmunks with each other. Siblings and same-sex chipmunks will not provide the desired litter, while unrelated chipmunks will have to be comfortable in each other's company before sexual behaviors are encouraged. Once impregnated, the female will have to be monitored to ensure that her nest box is protected from invasion by other cage mates.

Upon the birth of the chipmunk babies, it then becomes your responsibility to ensure that each individual pup receives the necessary amount of milk and attention from its mother, until it reaches a state of independence at eight weeks. It takes a successful combination of all the above elements to raise a healthy brood of babies that can then be kept as pets or sold to potential owners. Despite your best intentions, should any unfavorable circumstances persist in the environment during any part of the breeding process, you may lose one or even more of your babies to illness or death.

Breeding adult chipmunks requires little by way of preparation for mating, reserving all the hard work for the birth of the babies. The same cage used to house the chipmunks can also be used for mating purposes; additional housing requirements will only have to be made in case you are hand rearing the chipmunk puppies away from the mother. A pregnant and nursing mother's diet will have to be supplemented with calcium and Vitamin-D rich foods, while ensuring that she does not succumb to stereotypical behavioral disorders.

If you, as a caregiver, can devote extra time and personal attention towards the care of additional chipmunks, breeding the exotic pets may be a profitable option for you.

1. Breeding season and mating behaviors

As the breeding season approaches, female chipmunks are generally the first to signal their readiness to find a mate through the subtle swelling of their genitals. In fact, females are observed to enter a state of "heat" considerably earlier than the males, who may not become sexually active until early February, compared to the female's readiness in January or even late December. This occasional incompatibility of timings may mean that your female may be in heat for one, even two cycles before the males pursue her. Once male chipmunks are ready, subsequent mating rituals are carried out over a period of three days at intervals of 10-14 days during the season, and are often playful, aggressive and overt.

Pursuing male suitors

Whether housed with a single mate or among a group of suitors, a female chipmunk will begin the mating dance by luring the male in with a series of calls. Positioning herself at a vantage point such as a high spot in the cage, the female sings out to the males on the first day of the mating ritual, in correspondence with her ovulation. The female specifically uses the first day to send out inviting calls and will not accept any advances from male suitors until the next day. The male chipmunks that do try to approach females in heat are usually warded off with an aggressive series of swipes and scratches with their paws. The males usually use the first day to assess all females in heat, and compete amongst themselves to win the opportunity to mate.

Accepting male advances

On the second day, the female chipmunk undergoes a transformation, not only in her behavior, but also in her luring calls. With distinctive personalities, each female chipmunk has an individual mating call, be it a soft, long purring chirp, or a slightly high-pitched series of melodious squeaks. Mating calls on the second day are particularly persistent, often lasting through a major part of the female's waking hours. This series of calls lets the suitors know that she is ready to mate, and will be available for up to 48 hours. Upon being beckoned, the male chipmunk approaches the female to begin the final phase of courtship.

During this stage, which may occur anywhere between the second and third day, the male will literally pursue the female in a short yet frantic chase around the cage. This will culminate with the female finally allowing the male to mate with her. The male chipmunk usually signals his readiness to end the chase and begin mating by approaching the willing female with a swishing tail, and an inhaling sound that may be short and sharp, or soft and drawn out. Once they begin to mate, expect the adults to engage in a series of intercourse throughout the day, which often ends with the male leaving the scene due to exhaustion.

Exiting the state of heat

By the end of the third day, the female should be content and no longer in heat. As a signal, she will stop giving out mating calls, and will rebuke any advances from male suitors who may still want to mate. Female chipmunks usually resume behaviors displayed on the first day of the mating ritual, only becoming vocal if they haven't been impregnated within 15 days.

There may be instances in which a female chipmunk is rebuffed or ignored by her suitor after the pursuit. The male may even become bored with his companion after a few mating sessions. In case the female is still interested in the same mate, or hasn't been satiated, she will try to draw his attention back through such behaviors as rolling around the male and sniffing him repeatedly. She may even begin to produce her mating calls to arouse his interest. Such attempts are often eventually successful, with the rare female being rejected repeatedly by the male.

Common exceptional mating behavior patterns

In a community cage, a female who has been rejected may then try to attract the attention of other males. As a caregiver, should this instance occur, it becomes your responsibility to become more observant of the chipmunks. When a female chooses to pursue multiple males at once, her decision often results in the males succumbing to fights and petty displays of aggression. A possible consequence of this event may also be the emergence of an alpha male that becomes the sole breeding companion for females (while other males remain "bachelors").

Among the females, in an especially tight-knit group, there have been several instances in which the alpha female has been the only chipmunk to be impregnated. The other females often delegate themselves to the roles of nursing maids, and help to provide care for the newborn. This phenomenon, though common, is mostly observed among sister chipmunks and cage mates that were raised together. Not all females may be as supportive, and may attack the babies once they are born.

Some females may react negatively towards being rejected, and become aggressive towards all cage mates as a result. Other females may become overly hostile when in heat, only allowing males to approach them on the second day. Even in such cases, there is little guarantee that the mating may be successful. It is this temperamental nature that poses a challenge to guaranteed breeding each mating season.

As a breeder, you are likely to have the highest rate of success if you raise two unrelated chipmunks together, or introduce them as adults before the mating period. Possessing a curious disposition, unrelated males and females will quickly develop an interest in each other, often sniffing each other in curiosity and engaging in playful banter as a bonding exercise. Related chipmunks should never be allowed to mate, for fear of birth defects and deformities in resultant babies, and an imbalanced family dynamic among the chipmunks.

2.   Caring for the young
Care during the gestation period

Once your female has successfully mated with the male of her choice, she should become pregnant in the next 10 to 14 days. In case the mating has been unsuccessful, the female will simply go back to producing mating calls and seeking attention, after taking a break of about 14 days. It is often difficult to tell when a female chipmunk is pregnant, as the swelling of the belly is barely visible, and there is little change in her daily routines. Your chipmunk, however, will constantly provide subtle cues hinting at an ongoing pregnancy, such as:

•   Initial chirping when in heat followed by silence 10-14 days after mating,

•   Aggressive behavior towards male and even female cage mates such as vigilant guarding of her territory and food supply,

•   The addition of padding and other soft elements to her nest box, either from the common area, or stolen from other nest boxes,

•   Sudden, persistent grooming behaviors, such as itching and bathing.

•   Development of sudden, brief erratic behavior patterns, such as excess hoarding of food during late hours of the night, giving themselves extra exercise, developing a taste for foods they usually reject, or feeding excessively on chipmunk bread or cuttlefish bones.

The gestation period in a chipmunk lasts between 28 and 32 days, and premature or delayed births by a few days are not uncommon.

Most of the behavioral pregnancy signs can be observed within the first two weeks of pregnancy. Proper confirmation of the ongoing gestation period will only visibly appear around the third week, through physical changes. You will notice a subtle gain in weight around the third week, followed by abrupt weight gain and noticeably swollen nipples during the last five days of pregnancy.

Your female chipmunk will signal that she is ready to give birth about two to three days before the event. Early signs of readiness include increased exhaustion and fatigue, decreased activity around the cage, and a preference for her own nest box. On the actual day of birth, female chipmunks will prepare for the event in their own individual ways. Pet owners have observed some females inducing labor by becoming hyperactive and frantic, while others resume a stationary position in their nest box until it is time to give birth.

At the first signs of labor, female chipmunks will prepare to settle themselves in their nest box, usually by scratching and shifting the padding within to make it comfortable. This frenzied activity will be followed by a period of relative silence, which may last up to an hour or two; at the end, you will hear multiple tiny squeaks from the newly-born, announcing their own birth.

As soon as she births them, the mother chipmunk will clean away uterine matter and bathe the babies with her saliva. Born silent, the babies will usually let out their first sounds as they are being mopped up, and quieten down as they are put to rest.

Birth and emergence of the babies

Upon birthing her young, the mother chipmunk spends the next week or so completely in the company of her young. She will spend nearly a day, or even more, after the birth recuperating and will be nearly impossible to spot or approach. For the next seven to ten days, you may spot the mother emerging from the birth burrow or nest box to collect food or drink water, but such trips are often quick, short and sparse.

The babies themselves are born blind, without fur and unable to leave their breeding spots for the first seven weeks. During this time, they rely heavily on their caregiver for nutrition, as well as protection from other chipmunks. Depending on the dominant coloring patterns of your chipmunk, stripes will appear on the babies' bodies between 7 and 12 days of age.

This event is quickly followed by the growth of fur within a week. Your chipmunks will only open their eyes between the ages of 25 and 30 days, accompanied by the opening of the ear pockets. This ability to see and hear now enables them to leave their nest and learn adult behavioral patterns. If you allow the mother to rear the babies by herself, you may only see the babies after the initial 35-day period.

3.   Handling the babies

How you handle the newborn babies is largely dependent on your relationship with the chipmunk mother; this activity will also affect the relationship you form with the puppies. Most pet owners, breeders and fanciers choose one of two methods to raise and handle the young chipmunks: either by interacting with them via their mother, or by hand rearing them personally.

Interaction via the mother chipmunk

The best way to rear and handle a young one is often to interact with it while it is cared for by the mother. If the female chipmunk has a close bond with you, and is comfortable in your presence, she should allow you to touch the chipmunks as early as the first week - this, however, is not advisable. It is wisest to leave the babies with the mother for the first week, and introduce yourself to the young from the second week onwards.

If you are interacting with the babies through the mother, you do not need to enforce strict bonding time until the fourth week, once the babies' eyes have opened. Once the young chipmunks emerge from their nest boxes and observe their mother, they will likely gravitate towards you during feeding times. To help break the ice, you can carry out bonding exercises mentioned in the earlier chapter, such as gaining trust by offering treats, and holding the chipmunks in your clothes for some time a day. If the mother is friendly, and the babies are cooperative, you should be able to hold your young chipmunk for at least half an hour by the first week.

Hand-rearing the puppies

When you choose to hand-rear the puppies, you also take up the responsibility of feeding them and providing sufficient incubation until they develop into adults. To enable their trust, you will need to introduce yourself to the babies before they open their eyes, at about two weeks of age.

Your initial contact with the babies should be as sparse as possible, limited at first only to feeding times, and then escalating to bonding and playtime. Unable to see or regulate body temperature, puppies will sense your presence by your smell, feel and warmth of your touch. You should, ideally, begin by touching them for a brief minute or two for the first few days, and then progress to holding the puppies individually, gently in your grasp for five minutes or more. Since you will also handle the puppies while you feed them, these moments will also serve as trust-building exercises and help you bond with your pet.

Feeding the babies

If you have left your young chipmunks with the mother, she will provide the initial milk they need for about 3 to 4 weeks. Once the babies open their eyes and can move out of the nests, mothers hen gradually reduce the supply of milk until the babies are completely weaned - a process that takes between 6 and 7 weeks to achieve. If you are hand-rearing your puppies, however, or the mother is unable to provide milk, you will have to provide timely puppy formulations yourself.

A reputed and trusted puppy milk replacer brand known as Esbilac provides all the basic feeding necessities for your young ones. When prepared with care and administered correctly, this milk replacer will comfortably sustain your young ones until they are ready for solid foods. To feed your chipmunks:

• Stock a bunch of sterile 1cc syringes, and use these to feed your young chipmunks.

• Prepare the milk replacer formula by combining two parts of water for every part of formula. To supplement this replacer and help prevent diarrhea, add in 1/3 part yogurt.

• Warm the mixture very slightly before feeding the chipmunk.

• For the first two weeks, baby chipmunks will require 1 to 2 ml of the replacer at intervals of three hours.

• During each feeding, release the liquid very slowly into the chipmunk's mouth. Every 5 to 7 seconds, take a small pause to allow the young one to swallow the formula comfortably.

• Stop the feed when the baby stops drinking from the formula, even if it hasn't completed its dose. Avoid forcing your puppy to consume more milk than it is capable of.

• Between the third and fourth week, you will increase the dosage of replacer from 3 to 4 ml, and try to slip in a piece of soft fruit once the baby's' eyes have opened.

• Once the babies have been fed, allow them at least an hour to process and digest their food.

Weaning the puppies

Whether it is the mother who is raising the puppies or you who is hand-rearing them, six weeks of age is the perfect time to begin introducing your young ones to solid foods. Baby chipmunks will often begin sampling softer nuts, seeds and fruits found around the cage once they begin to leave the nest box. Learned by observing adult behavioral patterns, you will mostly involve yourself as a food source in order to bond with the chipmunk.

If you are letting the mother raise the babies, it is best not to separate them until the babies have been completely weaned, a process that may even take up to 10 weeks. You will be able to spot a fully weaned baby once they start actively foraging for food and stop relying on their mothers for companionship.

If you are hand-rearing the babies, you will introduce solid foods such as soft fruit and vegetables at six weeks, progressing to soft nuts and needs. At around eight weeks of age, your chipmunk should be able to crack open soft nuts independently, and will refuse the formula - a sure sign that it has been weaned successfully. In order to ensure that your young ones wean without incident or worry:

•   Prepare foods before feeding the puppies; peel, de-seed and chop fruits and vegetables, crack open hard nuts and soften tough seeds.

•   Cut up food into bite-size pieces that can comfortably be held by the puppies, but not swallowed or choked on in one bite.

•   Supplement the food with a bowl of water, shallow enough to prevent the chipmunk from falling into it and drowning.

If you have provided the right feeding and caring conditions, your chipmunks should make a successful transition from young ones to developing adults between the ages of eight and ten weeks. Do not expect all the puppies to develop at the same rate - they may wean, tame and become independent at their own pace, depending on their breed, parenting, handling, and individual natures. From ten weeks onwards, chipmunks will continue to develop and display personality traits such as dominance, aggression, sociability and loyalty. They will form bonds with their siblings, learn to forage and copied from their parents, and learn their place among larger groups of chipmunks.

From this point, until the chipmunks attain the age of ten months, younger siblings and their parents can live together in relative harmony in the same cage. The only instance in which parents may show adversity towards their young is if the mother is pregnant with a second litter, or if the young ones make too much noise during feeding, attracting the wrath of other female chipmunks.

Once they approach the ten-month mark, younger chipmunks will begin displaying signs of readiness to mate and breed. If left with their parents and other siblings, these signs could transition into incestuous breeding rituals or even competitive fighting for sexual dominance, especially between male adults and their sons. In such instances, it may be best to separate the chipmunks and introduce them to potential mates ahead of time. You can introduce them once again to the family members when the breeding season is complete, and the puppies have grown up.

Chapter 10: Chipmunks and Health-related Issues

If provided with the right care, timely checkups and a hygienic housing environment, most chipmunks will live their days in robust health, only affected in their old age by such ailments as organ failure or heart attacks. Most common infections and physical ailments can be traced to an imbalance in their diet, poor housing conditions or external psychological factors that indirectly impact the chipmunk's wellbeing.

A healthy chipmunk is alert, active and maintains a constant stream of activity throughout its waking hours. Chipmunks with no signs of infection will have clear eyes, with no discharge oozing from the nose or ears. A thick coat of fur is another characteristic sign of a healthy chipmunk; abrupt thinning or loss of fur is often an indicator of a larger physical irregularity. Not prone to laziness, any displays of lethargic behavior by your chipmunk should cause concern, especially if accompanied by other red flags.

1.   Critical Health Concerns
Metabolic Bone Disease

Metabolic Bone Disease is a common ailment caused among chipmunks that do not receive enough calcium and disproportionately large amounts of phosphorus in their diet. If left untreated, Metabolic Bone Disease, also known as MBD, may lead to the weakening of bones, seizures, and ultimately death.

An imbalance in the levels of calcium and phosphorus generally occurs when the chipmunks consume too many nuts and seeds, rich in phosphorus, but not in calcium. A low supply of vitamin D, essential for the absorption of calcium from food sources, may also be a contributing factor. If housed indoors with little or no exposure to sunlight, chipmunks rely solely on food for their supply of this vitamin; if given in small amounts, the chipmunk's system may be unable to break down calcium, even if it is supplied in healthy doses. Once affected, the symptoms and effects of MBD can take months of medication and rehabilitation to reverse, making prevention more essential than cure.

Common symptoms include increased periods of drowsiness and lethargy, decreased activity and willingness to exercise, unsteady gait, loss of appetite, noticeable frailty in bones, loss of fur, sudden bouts of seizures, and partial or complete paralysis. When touched, chipmunks with MBD may also be extremely cool to the touch - this is because MBD distorts the animal's ability to regulate body temperature, further weakening its health. Attempts at warming up the rodent on your part may take longer than usual, and may exhaust the pet.

Chipmunks should be taken to the veterinarian as soon as any symptoms of MBD are displayed. Depending on the severity of the condition, most pet experts will recommend a prolonged treatment with the calcium supplement Nutrobal or similar. If your chipmunk has already had seizures and may be on the verge of physical collapse or death, the veterinarian may even inject a direct dose of liquid calcium into the animal to help it survive therapy and treatment.

Nutrobal and other calcium supplements will have to be added to each feed in the recommended doses with a sterilized syringe. The pet will also have to be isolated from other cage mates, and kept in highly incubated conditions due to its inability to regulate body temperature. Heating bottles and pads can be warmed up and slid under the chipmunk's cage floor to help heat up the premises. Several pet owners also prescribe a pill of calcium carbonate, crushed and fed to the chipmunk via a syringe, to help replenish depleted levels.

Chipmunks affected with MBD also become dehydrated and are unable to feed themselves water during the initial phases of recovery. Water can also be fed to the pets with the help of syringes or bottle droppers, and supplemented with helpings of yogurt and puppy milk formula until the chipmunk is strong enough to feed itself.

Despite early signs of recovery, chipmunks who have had seizures during their encounter with MBD may still experience a fit once a week or less frequently for the next few months. It is best to monitor its health with the assistance of your local pet expert to help ascertain that the chipmunk's recovery is on the right track. If attended to immediately and given the right kind of rehabilitation, chipmunks can make a recovery from MBD in a span of eight weeks or even less.

Upper Respiratory Infection

Upper Respiratory Infections (URI) may not be as lethal to a chipmunk's health as MBD, but are highly contagious and will also affect the health of other chipmunks in the cage. Not caused by one sole virus, URI can arise from the chipmunk being exposed to a variety of inhospitable housing conditions, such as damp bedding, a sudden change in temperature, a rise in ammonia levels in the cage, an infection contracted from another cage mate, or accumulation of mold in their habitat that has not be cleaned away.

When affected, chipmunks will display such symptoms as exaggerated difficulty while breathing, accompanied by peculiar clicking noises. These noises may seem to occur at infrequent times at the start, but may become more consistent with the passage of time. This clicking sound occurs due to a blockage in the animal's' nasal passage or lungs, and prominent clicking sounds that occur with every breath could be indicative of a larger underlying respiratory infection. Other symptoms exhibited by a chipmunk affected with a URI include excessive shivering, prolonged periods of lethargy, loss of appetite and a subdued mood.

Since URIs are caused by unfavorable conditions in the chipmunk's environment, there are few medications that can directly help cure your pet. A veterinarian may be able to help alleviate discomfort and restore some lost health in the chipmunk by prescribing a treatment with an antibiotic known as Baytril for up to a week. Chipmunks often respond positively to Baytril and may seem to have made a recovery almost overnight, however it is best to continue the treatment following the veterinarian's orders to prevent a possible relapse.

Chipmunks who have been affected with URIs will need to be separated from their cage mates, and only returned when the housing conditions in their original cage are favorable. If the culprit behind the infection is an element within the cage, such as damp bedding or accumulated mold, other chipmunks will also have to be evacuated while the premises is disinfected and the bedding and flooring changed. Clothes worn during the disinfection process should also either be discarded or cleaned separate from other clothing; while chipmunks may not be able to pass on colds, viral strains from their infections could easily be transmitted to other susceptible organisms through such surfaces as clothing.

Tumors

Chipmunks may develop cancers of the skin and sexual organs, and may even be spotted with a tumor lump protruding through a spot on its ears, nose, mammary organs or testicles. Testicular and mammary cancer, in particular, can be particularly traumatic for your chipmunk, and may result in premature death if not diagnosed and removed from the body at once. Chipmunks may also contract brain cancer, first observable through sudden seizures and frothing at the mouth.

The tumors themselves are either may benign or malignant; your exotic pet expert will be able to determine the urgency and intensity of treatment upon diagnosis. In some cases, successful removal of a cancerous tumor may still not be able to prevent the infection from spreading to other parts of the body; in such cases, your pet expert will possibly suggest that you alleviate your pet's suffering by putting them down

Stroke, Heart Attack and other Cardiac Irregularities

Health concerns such as strokes and heart attacks are common among elderly chipmunks, and chipmunks who have undergone a particularly traumatic experience. While a heart attack may be caused by a variety of factors other than stress, including a poor diet or lack of exercise, the cause of strokes may sometimes be harder to isolate in captive chipmunks.

It is not instantly easy to tell when a chipmunk has suffered a stroke; in fact, it may take a few minutes of observation to determine. A stroke can often be spotted in its later stages, when the animal's head begins to tilt to one side during movement and exercise - indicating an imbalance and irregularity in distance judgment and depth perception.

A heart attack, on the other hand, is harder to spot, as your chipmunk will fall unconscious on the floor of the cage when affected with one. It is best to take your chipmunk to the veterinarian to help determine the best path of immediate action. Your chipmunk may also be susceptible to other heart problems, such as irregular heartbeats, palpitations and heart failure. Any cardiac irregularities will manifest externally as difficulty in breathing; if your pet shows any signs of labored breathing, a visit to the nearest veterinarian is of utmost importance.

Kidney and Liver Diseases

Chipmunks are able to maintain healthy kidneys and liver so long as you provide them with adequate drinking water on a daily basis. Hydration is also derived from fruits, vegetables and other food sources, making it almost impossible for chipmunks to experience failures of the kidneys and liver at an early age. If kidney and liver failure is experienced, it is usually observed among chipmunks that have reached a late age in their life cycle.

Failing kidneys and liver are first hinted at through increasingly frequent trips to the water feeder and a higher urination frequency. This inability to hold in urine is often indicative of a kidney that is no longer able to process excretory matter at its usual ability. Often irreversible without putting the chipmunk's life at risk, most veterinarians will suggest that you put your chipmunk down once its kidneys and liver begin to shut down.

Megaesophagus

Megaesophagus is not usually common among chipmunks, but when caused, can severely impact your pet's health and wellbeing. Characterized by an irregularity in the food pipe, a chipmunk with a megaesophagus will have lifelong difficulties feeding on solid foods, and will require dedicated lifelong care for it to survive.

Usually caused among younger chipmunks during the developmental stages, a megaesophagus restricts the passage of food from the tube into the stomach; it may also lead the food to make a detour and lodge itself in the lung area, causing aspiration. The inability to digest food properly may also affect the chipmunk's will to feed and drink water, indirectly impacting its weight and health.

Common symptoms that may hint at a megaesophagus include a loss of appetite, coughing, difficulty in swallowing and regurgitation of swallowed food. The chipmunk may also have difficulty in breathing, revealed by a clicking sound at constant intervals. Veterinarians will often prescribe Baytril to help alleviate breathing difficulties, but treatment will often only include a specific diet that suits the pet's delicate system.

Once diagnosed with megaesophagus, the chipmunk will have to be separated from cage mates; its weakened appearance and timid demeanor may cause other aggressive cage mates to bully or even attack it. Due to the inability to digest solid foods, all food will have to be mashed and pureed before feeding; you will also have to personally feed your chipmunk and monitor its chewing and swallowing habits to ensure that no food is choked on. Megaesophagus may be a lifelong ailment, but can be prevented from becoming life threatening to your chipmunk.

2. Prolonged Health Concerns
Epilepsy

Chipmunks are just as prone to brain seizures and epileptic attacks as other mammals such as humans or dogs. The intensity of the seizures may not always be consistent, neither may the frequency of each seizure; once an epileptic attack grips your chipmunk, however, the damage it causes may be irreversible.

Your veterinarian should be contacted at the first sign of a seizure. An epileptic episode may also hint at an underlying tumor in the brain, which will need to be extracted at the earliest. If the seizures have begun to appear at regular intervals, it often indicates that your chipmunk's mental health has deteriorated rapidly. In such instances, your veterinarian may recommend putting your pet to sleep; the most painless option in this circumstance.

Mastitis

Mastitis is a reproductive disease that will only affect your female chipmunks, often during or immediately after pregnancy. This does not, however, exclude the possibility of the development of mastitis during other times in a chipmunk's life.

A healthy female chipmunk will have mammaries that are equal in size, or only slightly disproportionate. When affected by mastitis, however, the mammary becomes engorged with infectious fluid and is often painful for the chipmunk to endure. When affected with mastitis immediately after pregnancy, female chipmunks may not want their teats to be touched, and may become hostile towards newly born offspring who rely on their mother's milk for survival. Your veterinarian will prescribe a course of antibiotics, along with an antiseptic topical cream to help treat the mother and keep her skin from becoming infected by germs from the feeding offspring.

Diabetes

As with many mammals that are fed an imbalanced diet that promotes obesity and excessive cholesterol with inadequate processing of sugar, chipmunks are also susceptible to such lifelong conditions as diabetes. Easy to identify with the passage of excessive urine and an amplified thirst, chipmunks that show possible symptoms of diabetes should be checked by their veterinarian to determine the earliest possible course of action. An altered diet and exercise habits may help increase the lifespan of your chipmunk, and prevent it from succumbing to organ failure.

Obesity

Excess weight and obesity can not only pose challenges to the amount of exercise your chipmunk receives, but could also be a gateway to such health-related issues as heart problems, diabetes and MBD. A few extra grams of weight on the chipmunk's body is needed to help it survive the colder winter months; if your chipmunk feeds on a diet that is high in sugar, sodium and fats, and receives disproportionately little exercise in return, it may be at risk of becoming unhealthily obese within a short span of time.

Chipmunks that are overweight often find it difficult to engage in such acrobatic activities as climbing, comfortable perching on high points, and somersaulting. Since such behaviors are typically characteristic of a chipmunk, any inability to perform such action may make your pet anxious and depressed. Obesity is best avoided by ensuring your pet receives a diet that has a balanced amount of fats, vitamins and minerals. A minimum of an hour of energetic exercise daily is equally important to help maintain optimum health and keep illnesses at bay.

3.   Common everyday ailments
Abscesses

In some cases, especially after your chipmunk has developed a dental infection or bitten itself on the inside of the mouth, an abscess may begin to form. Basically a swelling that fills up with pus, abscesses can be irritating for your chipmunk, and if left untreated, even lethal.

An abscess heals best when the thin outer film of skin is pierced to allow the fluid within to drain out. If your chipmunk bites on this skin, or scratches it in irritation, it's essential that the fluid not be swallowed or ingested. Infected pus from an abscess or even an untreated abscess can quickly spread the infection throughout the chipmunk's body, and result in such cases as blood poisoning. In the most severe cases, pus from a chipmunk's abscess has caused enough toxicity to result in cardiac or renal failure.

Abscesses will most often form around the mouth, sometimes in the insides of the cheeks pouches as well. As soon as your chipmunk begins showing signs of dental infection, or starts to attempt itching the affected area, take it to your exotic pet expert. For mild cases, it should be prescribed Baytril, a common antibiotic used to soothe such inflammations within a week. If the antibiotics fail to work, or the swelling needs immediate attention, your pet expert will advise a quick surgical procedure.

Draining the fluid is a simple matter of administering anesthetic to the chipmunk and releasing the toxic pus with a few simple moves. While antibiotics should often be all that's needed to help treat abscesses, it's best to take up recommendations for a surgical procedure to avoid any further complications.

Overgrown Teeth

Chipmunks have teeth that continue to grow for the duration of the animal's life. In the wild, chipmunks keep their teeth trimmed to the perfect length by gnawing on foods and substances with a tough coating, such as nuts, berries and wood chippings. As a caregiver for a tame chipmunk, it becomes your responsibility to provide objects that your pet can gnaw at. If such food or chew toys are not provided, your pet's teeth will grow and cover the lower teeth completely, making it difficult for your chipmunk to eat.

Overgrown teeth are a common dental issue faced by many chipmunk owners, especially those who are raising their first furry friend. This irregularity can be easily corrected with a simple procedure conducted at your veterinarian's office. If you are so inclined, you can also clip your chipmunk's teeth yourself, but be warned. This procedure, simple though it may be, is also one that requires great delicacy and alertness while clipping, so as not to hurt your pet or cause it duress. You also need to possess the skill of holding your chipmunk still or put it to sleep while you clip, and have the stomach to carry out this procedure - a feat your exotic pet expert has achieved with ample training. As a precautionary measure, you can incorporate toys with rough edges into your pet's routine, and supplement its feed with nuts and tough berries it can gnaw on.

Eye-related health concerns

Chipmunks have large, sensitive eyes that are easily agitated by a variety of irritants. Any signs of discharge or swelling from your pet's eyes immediately signal an inhospitable element in the environment, be it hay from the chipmunk's bedding, the fumes from scented air-sprays or even smoke emitted from burning cigarettes. In many instances, a watery or pus-like discharge could also be an outward manifestation of a respiratory infection.

Most commonly, you may find a watery or sticky, gummy discharge at the inner corner of your pet's eyes on some mornings. Similar to the matter that collects around the human eye during sleep, it can be cleaned away easily with a damp swab of cotton, and is no cause for concern. However, if your pet has a continuous discharge of fluid from either eye that persists for over three days, and has developed reddish marks around the eyes, you should contact your exotic pet expert immediately.

Other, more persistent eye problems your chipmunk may encounter could include conjunctivitis or cataract, either in one eye or both. Conjunctivitis can commonly be spotted by the red swelling in the chipmunk's eyes, accompanied by a watery discharge. If your chipmunk shares its cage with other mates, now is the time to isolate it in a separate disinfected cage until it recuperates completely. Your veterinarian will also be able to prescribe antibiotics to help treat your chipmunk.

Cataracts manifest themselves with a milky white coating on the surface of either or both eyes. This white, filmy layer may cover either a part of the eye, or the entire eye - rendering your chipmunk temporarily blind. Your pet expert should be contacted immediately to help conduct necessary surgical procedures and provide medication to treat the chipmunk.

As your chipmunk ages, it may begin to experience impaired visibility, eventually progressing to partial or complete blindness. A common phenomenon signaling old age, there is little you can do to reverse this process. Cataracts may also develop in an aging chipmunk's eyes, and your pet expert should be able to advise whether a surgical procedure is safe.

To help keep your pet's exposure to eye and chest infections down, here are some precautionary measures you can take:

• Keep your chipmunk away from potential allergens such as sawdust and damp hay. Provide dry hay padding, changed on a regular basis, and fill the cage with such materials as bark shavings and chippings, or wood kitty litter.

• Avoid spraying heavily fragranced air fresheners around your pet's cage. Chipmunks are relatively odorless pets and will not stink up their atmosphere. More importantly, the chemicals within the sprays could irritate and infect your pet's eyes, even chest.

• Passive smoke from cigarettes and other tobacco-products are just as harmful to your pet's eyes and respiratory system. Avoid smoking in the same room as the chipmunk's cage.

• If your chipmunk is experiencing blindness due to aging or cataracts, help them find their way around the environment by keeping the contents of the cage in the same positions. Chipmunks can isolate and remember the positions of items in their vicinity, but you if shift the contents around, it may confuse and even cause distress to the chipmunk.

4.   Behavioral issues

A sudden occurrence of irregularity in the behavior of chipmunks is often the external manifestation of a low sense of emotional wellbeing. Caused by unfavorable housing conditions, a sudden shift in daily routines or an unpleasant addition to the pet's environment, behavioral disorders, if left unchecked, can cause a significant shift in your chipmunk's personality.

Stereotypical Behavior Patterns

Stereotypical behavior patterns are defined by a constant, repetitive action undertaken by a chipmunk that may not be compatible with its regular behavioral patterns. Some chipmunks exhibit such stereotypical behaviors as running around a rodent wheel in endless circles (if one is placed in the cage); others may burrow at a frantic pace with no end in sight, while yet other chipmunks may perform acrobatic feats such as somersaults without a pause.

If spotted, these erratic behavior patterns will often result from the chipmunk's dissatisfaction with its housing conditions and the exercise provided. As active rodents, chipmunks require ample space within the cage to exercise, along with the opportunity to wander outside the cage to alleviate boredom. In the absence of external exercise motivators, chipmunks tend to find a single activity that amuses them, which is first practiced sporadically, but then increases in frequency at an alarming rate.

Stereotypical behaviors, once ingrained in the chipmunk's routine, can be difficult and sometimes impossible to break. In many cases, these behaviors will lead to the chipmunk exercising itself to exhaustion. If your chipmunk exhibits erratic stereotypical behavior patterns, it is wise to consult with your veterinarian to find an exotic pet rehabber. Other solutions may include changing the cage for a larger, more spacious one (if a small age is the root cause), and giving your pet extra time to exercise, along with an assortment of new toys with which to occupy themselves.

Stress and Shock

Stereotypical behavior patterns may not only be an indicator of displeasure with exercise; in many cases, a stereotypical behavior often points towards a larger stressor in the chipmunk's environment. With exact demands that need to be fulfilled consistently, chipmunks may be exposed to a number of stressors on a daily basis that may put their emotional well being at risk.

The introduction of new cage mates is among the most common cause of stress in chipmunks previously housed in isolation. Aggressive cage mates, parents or offspring may also traumatize a timid and reclusive pet. Chipmunks feel equally threatened by larger animals; any pets that are allowed around the chipmunks and attempt to pursue the rodents will cause them stress.

Known to have extremely sensitive ears, chipmunks often react negatively when exposed to the cathode rays emitted by television sets. While constant flickering light may be too harsh on their sensitive eyes, long exposure to television sets can stress the chipmunks out due to a constant barrage of unexpected and unfamiliar sounds.

Entering a state of shock is known to be extremely lethal to a chipmunk's wellbeing. If not provided with immediate attention, a traumatic state has known to result in a chipmunk's death in as little as a few hours after being exposed to the stressor. Chipmunks may also enter a state of shock when stricken with severe health ailments such as Upper Respiratory Infections and Mastitis. It is wise to separate a chipmunk that has entered a state of shock from other cage mates (if housed in a group) and give it medical attention at the earliest. A few days of solitary rehabilitation, accompanied by extra attention and timely food can help return your chipmunk back to its healthy state.

5.   Administering treatments to the chipmunk

Chipmunks are not the easiest pets to administer medication to. Largely thanks to their aversion towards touching or grabbing, and also owing to their tiny mouths, any medication has to be transferred into the chipmunk's mouths with care and a little creativity.

Most medication prescribed for your chipmunks are available in liquid form, and can be transferred into your pet's mouth with the help of a syringe. Your pet should also be willing to let you feed it medicine. In case your chipmunk turns out to have a stubbornly resistant attitude towards the syringe, you can try sneaking the medicine into their favorite food items.

Most antibiotics can easily be injected into small fruit pieces, or can even be mixed with a spoon of peanut butter or honey - snacks that many chipmunks seem to favor. You can also add medicines to your pet's water or mix it with a small serving of fresh fruit juice to make it appetizing to your pet.

No matter what antibiotics you may have to feed your chipmunk, it is important to remember that these medications (especially Baytril, a commonly-prescribed medicine for chipmunks) can be very harsh on your pet's digestive system. The chemical composition of the antibiotics has been formulated to kill all possible sources of infection, and could kill the good bacteria in the chipmunk's intestines. To help prevent further complications from arising due to strong medications, supplement your chipmunk's medicine with a small serving of yogurt. A spoon or two of the healthy probiotic food is not only delicious for most chipmunks, but will also restore healthy bacteria and soothe your chipmunk's intestinal tract.

Treating minor cuts and wounds:

Apart from feeding antibiotics to your chipmunks, treatments are also administered by way of gentle bathing to treat injuries like cuts and wounds. As with the case of feeding oral medication, it is essential that your chipmunks are comfortable with your presence and handling of them before you try to bathe them. If they react aggressively towards your advances, it may only serve to aggravate their injuries.

Cuts and superficial wounds are best treated with some lukewarm water and salt. To effectively treat your chipmunk:

• Combine just a pinch or two of salt into the water, and pour this mix into a small bottle with a spray top.

• Gently shake the contents before spraying it onto the affected area.

• Once the cut or wound is adequately wet with the solution, apply a layer of antiseptic spray over the area. Antiseptic sprays used to treat superficial injuries for humans will work just as well on chipmunks.

• You can also substitute the antiseptic spray for antiseptic wipes, if they are available. Gently wipe the affected area to disinfect the wound.

• No matter how little the injury or cut, it is best to monitor its healing, and contact your exotic pet expert in case the injury worsens or becomes infected.

• Your veterinarian will most likely prescribe Colloidal Silver as a treatment for wounds inflicted on your chipmunk. While effective, Colloidal Silver does not mix well with water on its own and it cannot be applied directly to the affected area. It is best mixed with other prescribed antibiotics and administered accordingly.

Your chipmunk may sometimes show signs of slight illness or may become stressed due to abrupt changes in its vicinity, such as an attack attempt by another pet, an attempt on your part to hold it, sudden injury, etc. In such cases, you can quickly calm your agitated chipmunk down with a simple squirt of Rescue Remedy spray. Essentially manufactured for human use, it is compatible with all other chipmunk medication, and pet owners have found this spray to be effective at soothing a frazzled chipmunk. Simply spray a tiny amount of Rescue Remedy behind the ears on the feet of your chipmunk. Hitting important nerve points on contact, the spray acts quickly to calm your pet down.

Knowing when to seek external medical assistance

Most illnesses and ailments that will affect your chipmunk will likely be caused by an imbalance in their diet, improper housing conditions or stress caused by external factors. As exotic pets, hardy though they may be, chipmunks are prone to a higher number of illnesses and infections owing to the difference between the conditions of captive environments and their natural habitat. This means that you will have to devote more time towards providing health care for a chipmunk than you would a dog or a cat.

In many cases, superficial wounds and infections can be treated at home, without seeking medical assistance. As long as your chipmunk is alert, active and not displaying signs of stress, medical attention may need consist of no more than separating the pet from cage mates for two or three days and providing the right medicine for the sickness.

A minor cold or injury, however, should not affect the behavior or daily routine of your chipmunk in any drastic way. Chipmunks will only act erratically and display signs of physical discomfort when they have been affected by a serious underlying medical condition. In such cases, it becomes important to contact your veterinarian at the earliest.

If your chipmunk is in need of urgent expert medical attention, it will display such signs as:

- Frothing at the mouth,

- A seizure episode,

- Partial or complete paralysis,

- Sudden and constant discharge from the eyes or ears,

- Loss of toe, or partial or complete limb or tail (due to injury).

Your chipmunk may not always display signs that are physical manifestations of an underlying illness. In some cases, illnesses such as Metabolic Bone Disease and Respiratory infections may only be hinted at by observing the chipmunk's physical signs for 24-48 hours. If your chipmunk displays the following signs for over 48 hours, it is best to rush it to your exotic pet expert at the earliest:

- Loss of appetite and thirst,

- Shedding and loss of fur,

- Abnormally frequent urination,

- Constant seizure episodes,

- Dull, listless behavior.

## 6.	Safeguarding your chipmunks against illnesses

If you are the type of pet owner who is loving, considerate and dedicated, then you most likely will already have a caregiving system that is mindful of your chipmunk's needs. In an ideal environment that gives the exotic the right type of food, housing and hygiene conditions, there is little chance that your pet will incur anything more serious than the odd fight-related injury.

Even so, it is always best to take every precaution necessary to safeguard your chipmunk against the possibility of illness and disease. Not only are diseases physically draining for the chipmunk, but several infections sustained by these rodents may also infect other cage mates. Here are a few ways by which you can ensure the health and well being of your pet:

1.	A daily cleaning of your chipmunk's cage tray is not only preferable, but is also essential. As adults, these animals eat generously, shed equally copious amounts of excrement, and create a mess with their burrowing and scampering habits that could quickly contaminate an enclosed space.

2.	Any kind of food that could decay and compost, along with all the excrement, should be cleaned out once daily.

3.	In addition to cleaning the tray, the bedding and flooring within the cage will also have to be replaced once every two to three months. This will avoid the possibility of any infestations from rotting matter.

4.   It is best to avoid putting in such items as small, easy-to swallow stones, twigs, gravel and allergens such as sawdust into the cage. Since chipmunks are curious creatures, they may try to eat objects they do not understand, leading to possible choking hazards and internal injuries.

5.   Chipmunks thrive best when housed in comfortable temperatures and conditions that mimic their natural surroundings. They become easily stressed if the climate in their cage is either susceptible to erratic changes, or is beyond their adaptability range. As mammalian creatures, consistent room temperature in the summer months, and slightly warmer nesting rooms in the winter months will keep your chipmunks safe from hypothermia and pneumonia.

6.   Keep a keen eye on the interaction of your chipmunks with other cage mates, members in the house and its immediate surroundings. Chipmunks are expressive by nature and will display stereotypical behaviors or visible signs of trauma when faced with injury or a perceived threat.

7.   Finally, closely monitor your feeding role as a caregiver, along with the amount of food needed by your chipmunks. While they do not need much to be healthy, chipmunks do require a constant source of healthy food and exercise in order to keep illness at bay.

7.   Providing insurance for your chipmunk

Animals such as chipmunks are referred to as exotics since they require specific standards for housing, diet and health care in order to live a long life without any medical complications. Despite your best intentions, you may not always be able to provide the daily care that chipmunks require; it is difficult to tell exactly how many nuts and seeds are right for their daily diet, or it may be difficult to replicate the conditions needed for hibernation and torpor, for example.

It is perhaps because of reasons like these that when chipmunks do succumb to illnesses, they are often of a recurring nature and require long-term care. A chipmunk that contracts a respiratory infection may have a weak immune system and may be constantly susceptible to infections; another pet with weak kidneys may constantly need medical attention. Providing veterinary care for each ailment that befalls your chipmunk can quickly become an expensive affair.

To help protect you financially, countries like the United States and the United Kingdom offer health insurance policies for pets of many varieties, including exotic small mammals such as chipmunks. Healthcare and medical plans chalked up by these companies provide an umbrella of financial cover for such cases as tooth ailments, kidney, liver and heart diseases, intestinal diseases, rectal issues, vaccinations and even cancer.

In the United States, pet insurance policies are offered by such companies as GoPetPlan and Embrace Pet Insurance. In the United Kingdom, you can find pet insurance policies with companies like Exotic Direct and Cliverton.

Conclusion

Now that you are equipped with all the information that you need with regards to chipmunks, I am sure that you will make a great owner. It is a lot of work to keep chipmunks at home. While that may sound intimidating, if you are unable to match all the requirements and needs of your exotic pets, you will only compromise on their health and well-being. To conclude, I would like to remind you that a chipmunk is a big financial commitment.

Here is a breakdown of the approximate costs of keeping a Chipmunk:

- Cage: $185 to $425 or £120 to £275

- Bedding: $6 to $30 or £4 to £20

- Feed: $4 to $10 or £3 to £7 for a 2-pound bag

- Feeder: $3 to $10 or £52to £7

- Water-feeder: $3 to $10 or £2 to £7

- Nesting box: $20 or £10

- Accessories: $40 to $150 or £20 to £230

Once you are sure of making this commitment, you can convert your home into a great place for your Chipmunks.

I hope this book answers all your questions about having Chipmunks.

References

All the websites mentioned in this book can provide a host of additional information on how to successfully raise chipmunks, through breeder-run websites and community pet owner forums.

At the time of writing, all the following links were active and functional; in the event that any source should re-direct you to an inactive page, please understand that the maintenance of these websites is subject to Internet-policies and the preferences of the website owners; we cannot claim personal responsibility for the same.

http://www.super-chipmunks.co.uk/

https://animalcorner.co.uk

http://www.petcare.org.uk

http://www.havahart.com

https://en.wikipedia.org

http://animaldiversity.org

http://www.nhptv.org

http://www.rspca.org.uk

http://www.paw-talk.net

http://ehealthforum.com

http://blog.nwf.org

http://animals.mom.me/

http://chiptastic.webs.com

http://chirpiechipmunkz.webs.com

http://www.moidilandia.com

http://www.mismatch.co.uk

http://www.mattbrundage.com

http://www.pets4homes.co.uk

http://www.ehow.com

http://modernpets.webs.com

http://www.outwitcritters.com

http://www.buzzle.com

http://www.orphanedwildlifecare.com

http://www.petcaregt.com

http://cheekychipmunksse.webs.com

http://ktarcus.hubpages.com

http://www.fcps.edu

http://www.esf.edu

http://www.pet-insurance-university.com

http://www.bornfreeusa.org

http://www.state.nj.us/health

Printed in Great Britain
by Amazon